CONTENTS

PREFACE

York Notes are designed to give you a broader perspective on works of literature studied at GCSE and equivalent levels. With examination requirements changing in the twenty-first century, we have made a number of significant changes to this new series. We continue to help students to reach their own interpretations of the text but York Notes now have important extra-value new features.

You will discover that York Notes are genuinely interactive. The new **Checkpoint** features make sure that you can test your knowledge and broaden your understanding. You will also be directed to excellent websites, books and films where you can follow up ideas for yourself.

The **Resources** section has been updated and an entirely new section has been devoted to how to improve your grade. Careful reading and application of the principles laid out in the Resources section guarantee improved performance.

The **Detailed summaries** include an easy-to-follow skeleton structure of the story-line, while the section on **Language and style** has been extended to offer an in-depth discussion of the writer's techniques.

The Contents page shows the structure of this study guide. However, there is no need to read from the beginning to the end as you would with a novel, play or poem. Use the Notes in the way that suits you. Our aim is to help you with your understanding of the work, not to dictate how you should learn.

Our authors are practising English teachers and examiners who have used their experience to offer a whole range of **Examiner's secrets** – useful hints to encourage exam success.

The General Editor of this series is John Polley, Senior GCSE Examiner and former Head of English at Harrow Way Community School, Andover.

The author of these Notes is Clare Findlay who gained a BA at Royal Holloway, and has been examining English since 1970. She was Head of English at St Anne's High School, Wolsingham, Co. Durham and currently teaches adults in Basic Skills and the Trinity Certificate for T.E.S.O.L.

The text used in these Notes is the Penguin Classics edition, 1996, edited by David Carroll.

PART ONE

INTRODUCTION

HOW TO STUDY A NOVEL

A novelist starts with a story that examines a situation and the actions of particular characters. Remember that authors are not photographers, and that a novel never resembles real life exactly. Ultimately, a novel represents a view of the world that has been created in the author's imagination.

There are six features of a novel:

❶ THE STORY: this is the series of events, deliberately organised by the writer to test the characters

❷ THE CHARACTERS: the people who hae to respond to the events of the story. Since they are human, they can be good or bad, clever or stupid, likeable or detestable, etc. They may change too!

❸ THE VIEWPOINT/VOICE: who is telling the story. The viewpoint may come from one of the characters, or from an omniscient (all-seeing) narrator, which allows the novelist to write about the perspectives of all the characters.

❹ THE THEMES: these are the underlying messages, or meanings, of the novel

❺ THE SETTING: this concerns the time and place that the author has chosen for the story

❻ THE LANGUAGE AND STYLE: these are the workds that the author has used to influence our understanding of the novel.

To arrive at the fullest understanding of a novel, you need to read it several times. In this way, you can see how all the choices the author has made add up to a particular view of life, and develop your own ideas about it.

The purpose of these York Notes is to help you understand what the novel is about and to enable you to make your own interpretation. Do not expect the study of a novel to be neat and easy: novels are chosen for examination purposes, not written for them!

CHECK THE BOOK

For more information about the author, check *George Eliot: A Life* published by Penguin (1997).

AUTHOR – LIFE AND WORKS

1819 Born, near Worcester, as Mary Ann Evans

1837 Death of her beloved mother

1841 Moves to Coventry where she meets a group of free thinkers and develops strong anti-religious feelings

1842 Refuses to attend church

1844 Works as a translator

1849 Death of her father

1851 Assistant editor of the radical *Westminster Review*; meets writer George Henry Lewes

1852–4 Lives at 142 The Strand, London a kind of intellectual lodging-house

1854 Scandalises polite society by moving in with Lewes who is a married man

1857 Writes *Scenes of Clerical Life*

1859 Her first novel *Adam Bede* is published and is critically acclaimed as a masterpiece

1861 *Silas Marner* is published

1863 *Romola* is published

1866 *Felix Holt, The Radical* is published

1871–2 *Middlemarch* published

1874–6 *Daniel Deronda* published

1878 Lewes dies

1880 Marries John Walter Cross

1880 Dies and is buried in Highgate, beside Lewes

1885 Cross's biography of George Eliot published

CONTEXT

1732–92 Sir Richard Arkwright invents mechanical loom

1750–1850 Industrial Revolution

1784–1809 Edmund Cartwright develops the power loom

1791 The death of John Wesley

1793–1815 The Napoleonic Wars

1807 Abolition of the slave trade

1833–50 Factory acts restrict the hours worked by women and children

1834 Poor Law Amendment Act attempts to tackle the problems of a fast-growing population

1857 Matrimonial Causes Act makes divorce easier

1870 The Married Women's Property Act allows a woman to retain £200 of her own earnings

1878 Matrimonial Causes Act allows a woman to separate from her husband

SETTING AND BACKGROUND

GEORGE ELIOT'S BACKGROUND

George Eliot was born as Mary Ann Evans at Arbury Farm, Warwickshire, in 1819, to Robert Evans and his second wife, Christiana. She was the youngest of their three children and her father's favourite. He had two older children from his first wife.

DID YOU KNOW?
This area was used in her description of Raveloe.

Shortly after Mary Ann's birth, the family moved to Griff House between Coventry and Nuneaton. Her father managed an estate in the rich farming countryside.

An unattractive child, Mary Ann was outstandingly clever, and devoted to her brother Isaac (born 1816). Their relationship was described in young Maggie Tulliver's love for her brother Tom in *The Mill on the Floss*.

Like Eppie, Mary Ann began her early education at a dame school. In 1824 she was sent away to school and was most unhappy. From 1828, she was in a school at Nuneaton, where she excelled in music and at classical and modern languages. Her education was unusual for a girl at that time. She was greatly influenced by her teacher, Maria Lewis, whose strong evangelical and Calvinistic beliefs she enthusiastically adopted. These were described in the church at Lantern Yard.

CHECK THE BOOK
The Mill on the Floss would be an excellent novel to compare and contrast with *Silas Marner*.

By 1837, her mother was dead. Mary Ann had left school and was housekeeper to her father. Influenced by liberal free thinkers like Charles and Caroline Bray, whom she met after her move to Coventry in 1841, she had an extreme reaction to Christianity. Her father refused to speak to her until she agreed to behave respectably and attend church.

From 1844 she worked as a translator and by 1851 was unpaid assistant editor of a periodical the *Westminster Review*. Her father's death in 1849 made her financially independent.

Through her publishing work she met many prominent English, American and European writers. These included the lively G.H. Lewes who had separated from his wife. Legal conditions at that

DID YOU KNOW?
Silas Marner grew from a childhood memory of a weaver with his bag.

time prevented a divorce. He and Mary Ann (now Marian) caused a scandal, at first bringing social exclusion, by living together until his death in 1878. Her brother Isaac ended all family contact until she married J.W. Cross, a man twenty years her junior, in 1880.

Persuaded by Lewes to write fiction, she was immediately successful. She published *Scenes of Clerical Life* in 1857 under the name of George Eliot. By using this male name, she hoped to protect her work and its sales from biased criticism because of her personal life and also from the dismissive attitude of the literary critics of the time towards female novelists. Like *Adam Bede* (1859), all her early books, including *Silas Marner* (1861), make use of her early life in Warwickshire to provide ideas and exact details of everyday country events.

George Eliot started *Romola* but interrupted it to write *Silas Marner*. Published in 1863, *Romola* was an historical novel set in fifteenth-century Florence. *Felix Holt* followed in 1866. This political novel was set in a period of change in English life – the 1832 Parliamentary Reform Act; George Eliot had lived through this period herself as a child. *Middlemarch*, published in 1872 but set in the same period as *Felix Holt*, was *A Study in Provincial Life*, according to its subtitle – again, this refers back to the countryside of her childhood. Regarded as George Eliot's best work, *Middlemarch* portrays the different interests and characters to be found in a small town and its surrounding countryside. Her last novel presented the Jewish *Daniel Deronda* (1876).

DID YOU KNOW?
In 1978, a memorial stone to George Eliot was erected in Poet's Corner, Westminster Abbey.

It is typical of all George Eliot's characters that they develop psychological insight into themselves and their moral position as they make their decisions.

AN ERA OF CHANGE

George Eliot began writing *Silas Marner* in autumn 1860. England was ending a century which had brought enormous changes in every area of life. Among the changes – there were many others – we find:

- The Industrial Revolution changed methods of production

- Factories were created

- The rise of great industrial towns

- A massive population shift

- Society changed from mainly agricultural to mainly industrial

- Attitudes about work, religion and government changed

The novel is striking for what it does not mention in its time span (c.1790–1820). Many major issues, including the following and many others, were ignored:

- The French Revolution and its effects

- The loss of America

- The abolition of the slave trade

- Catholic emancipation

- Riots – from varied causes

- Many repressive laws – including suspension of habeas corpus and the Anti-Combination Acts

- India

The Napoleonic Wars (1793–1815) against France had widespread effects but only one is mentioned in *Silas Marner* – the economic effect on farming:

- Eppie came to Silas during 'that glorious war-time' (Ch. 3, p. 23) when the high price of food made farmers rich.

- She marries when peace has brought the 'increasing poor-rate and the ruinous times' (Ch. 17, p. 151) which upset Mr Lammeter and Godfrey.

Another topical cause of great unrest, urban social conditions, is mentioned in Chapter 21 when Silas and Eppie try to visit Lantern Yard. The vast changes brought by the Industrial Revolution caused hardship to many and led to riots. The hardship is hinted in the description of the 'great manufacturing town' (Ch. 21, p. 177) and a 'dark ugly place' (Ch. 21, p. 178). Indeed, Eppie can hardly believe 'any folks lived i' this way, so close together' (Ch. 21, p. 178).

 DID YOU KNOW?
George Eliot recreated old-fashioned village life to contrast industrial values and conditions.

 CHECK THE NET
Search the Internet to find out more about the laws of the time.

Before the opening of the novel (c.1800) Silas had worked in the town which he is unable to recognise thirty years later; so he stops 'several persons in succession' (Ch. 21, p. 178) to check its name.

The contrast with the pleasantly situated and 'important-looking' (Ch. 1, p. 7) village of Raveloe, with its closely knit and co-operative community, is shown by Eppie's 'distress' when she visits Lantern Yard. She is 'ill at ease' with the 'multitude of strange indifferent faces' (Ch. 21, p. 178). The people are not interested in strangers. Unlike Raveloe, there is little curiosity in people or events.

Silas feels ill with shock that Lantern Yard has been replaced by 'that big factory' (Ch. 21, p. 179), but the brush-maker arrived 'only ten years ago' (Ch. 21, p. 179) and cannot help with information.

WHY IS SETTING IMPORTANT?

Setting is often vital to a novel's plot or action. National and international events influence the lives, thoughts, attitudes and actions of people living through them. The book's characters live inside its action or plot and are affected by the existing mental and physical conditions of their period and place.

The setting makes boundaries for the story. Look for the clues which create:

- The historical date or period when the story happens

- Where the events happen

Silas Marner is set in the countryside and in a village community almost untouched by events elsewhere. The effects of the Industrial Revolution do not affect Silas until he is 'Fifty-five, as near as I can say' (Ch. 19, p. 167), when 'the weaving was going down' (Ch. 16, p. 141) following the spread of the powered loom, invented by Cartwright in 1794.

George Eliot works hard on the details of her settings so that you can imagine or visualise people and events. For example, Raveloe lay 'in a rich central plain … nestled in a snug well-wooded hollow, quite an hour's journey on horseback from any turnpike' (Ch. 1, p. 7). It is

EXAMINER'S SECRET

When you make notes on topics always include quotations (and the page number) to back-up your points. It is easier if you do this as you go along rather than just before the exam!

'important-looking', had 'two or three large brick-and-stone homesteads ... standing close upon the road' and has 'well-walled orchards and ornamental weathercocks' (Ch. 1, p. 7). Such detail gives us Raveloe's geographical position, atmosphere and period.

Raveloe was typical of any village before the Industrial Revolution. Its class structure is shown through:

- Village customs and leisure – the Rainbow, Christmas and New Year parties

- Travel – gentry and other people

- Dress – gentry and others (notice how details reveal class)

- Religion: town – chapel, artisan class, Calvin / Wesley; country – church, Rector (Mr Crackenthorpe), Parish clerk (Mr Macey), Deputy (Mr Tookey) and others

Social class is based on housing (contrast Red House and Silas's cottage), land ownership, work (contrast town and country trades and the difference between Squire Cass and the other farmers), health and social care and education.

As you read *Silas Marner*, try to keep notes on these topics – it will make your essay writing and revision for any examination much easier.

EXAMINER'S SECRET
Always make full use of the details provided by the author such as details about Raveloe in Chapter 1 or the gentry in Chapter 3.

Now take a break!

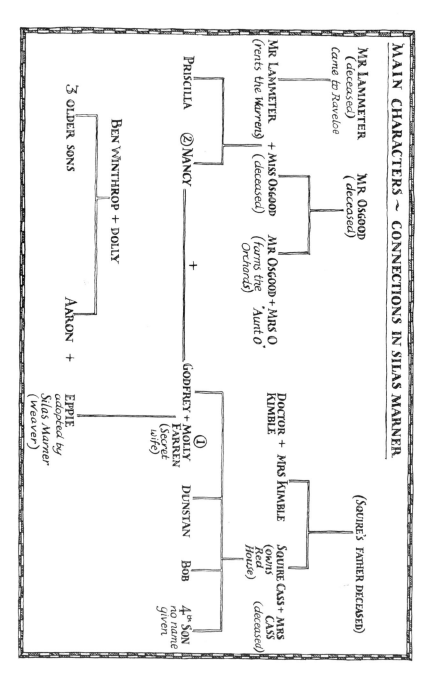

MAIN CHARACTERS ~ CONNECTIONS IN SILAS MARNER

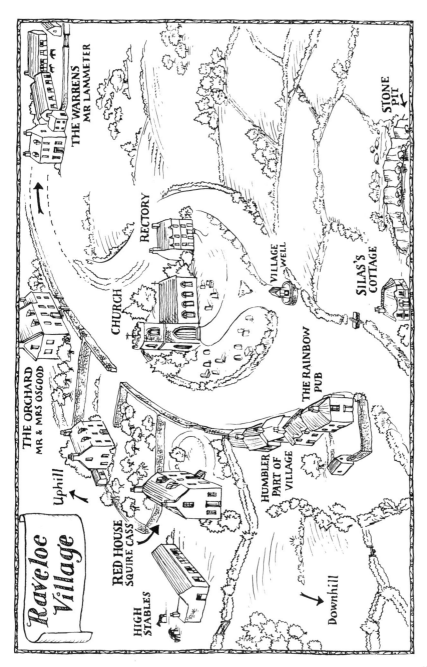

1

Silas leaves Lantern Yard after he is falsely accused of the theft of Church money. The true culprit is his friend who wants Silas out of the church so that he can marry Sarah, Silas's fiancée.

2

Silas moves to Raveloe, a distant village where, for fifteen years, he works as a lone weaver. He no longer attends church and is treated as an outsider. His life revolves around counting the money he earns.

3

Godfrey Cass, son of the village squire, is in trouble with his father over an unpaid debt. Godfrey has used the money to pay his unpleasant younger brother, Dunstan, to keep quiet about his marriage to Molly Farren.

4

Dunstan blackmails his brother into giving him a horse to sell for more money. He accidentally kills the horse and steals Silas's gold. Dunstan subsequently disappears. The theft remains unsolved.

5

Godfrey tells his father part of the story about the money, whilst not revealing that he has married Molly. His father disowns Dunstan and decides that he will try to marry off Godfrey to Nancy Lammeter, a wealthy local.

6

Silas becomes withdrawn after the theft and the villagers regard him as mad. He is effectively a broken man since his gold represented his only interest in life.

7

At the New Year's Eve ball at the Squire's hall, Nancy does not discourage Godfrey's interest. At precisely the same time Molly is dying of exposure as she brings her child to expose Godfrey's past.

8

The child finds its way to Silas's house where he claims her as his own. Godfrey, faced with the chance to claim the child, refuses to do so, and Silas becomes the adoptive father of Hephzibah, or Eppie as she is known.

9

Sixteen years have passed. Godfrey has married Nancy. When Dunstan's body is found, finally ending the mystery of the theft, Godfrey reveals his secrets to Nancy. As they are childless she agrees to ask Silas to give them Eppie.

10

Faced with a choice of fathers, Eppie unhesitatingly chooses Silas. Despite his disappointment, Godfrey continues to give financial support to Eppie though he decides that his fatherhood is a secret that he will not reveal publicly.

11

Silas revisits Lantern Yard with Eppie in an effort to set the record straight. The chapel has disappeared along with its parishioners to be replaced by a large factory. Time has moved on.

12

Eppie marries her childhood sweetheart, Aaron Winthrop, at a wedding paid for by Godfrey Cass. He is unavoidably detained elsewhere but the happy couple return to their cottage which has been altered and extended by Godfrey.

PART TWO

SUMMARIES

GENERAL SUMMARY

CHAPTERS 1–3: SILAS MOVES TO RAVELOE AND WE MEET THE CASSES

 CHECK THE BOOK

If you have enjoyed George Eliot's short, simple *Silas Marner*, an interesting follow-on would be to read her longer, more complex *Middlemarch* (Penguin Classics, 1994 – first published 1871). This is often considered her best novel and like *Silas Marner* is set in a country environment in the first half of the nineteenth century. This is also available as a BBC video (1994).

Around 1805, a linen-weaver, Silas Marner, moves to a cottage outside Raveloe. He works long hours and is antisocial. The villagers' fear of Silas increases and, after helping Sally Oates, he refuses to aid anyone through his herbal knowledge.

Raveloe is a very different world from the northern town where Silas grew up and belonged to a strict religious group. Silas suffers from fits and his friend, William Dane, had taken advantage of this to frame Silas for theft. Silas was expelled from his church. His fiancée, Sarah, had ended their engagement and married William.

Squire Cass is a bad father and landlord. His oldest son, Godfrey, is blackmailed into giving his tenant's rent to Dunstan – the Squire's second son. Dunstan threatens to tell the Squire of Godfrey's secret marriage to Molly Farren, and refuses to repay the rent. He persuades Godfrey to sell Wildfire – his horse.

CHAPTERS 4–10: A THEFT, A DISAPPEARANCE AND VILLAGE CONCERNS

Before Dunstan can sell Wildfire, the horse dies during a hunt. As Dunstan walks home, he sees Silas's cottage and decides to 'borrow' the weaver's gold. The cottage is empty and, quickly finding the hidden gold, Dunstan steals it and disappears.

Silas discovers his beloved gold is missing and rushes to the Rainbow for help. Meanwhile, uninterested in the missing Dunstan, the Squire urges Godfrey to propose to Nancy Lammeter.

Silas's misery changes the villagers' attitude to him. Among others, Dolly Winthrop visits and invites Silas to church.

CHAPTERS 11–15: THE FATEFUL NEW YEAR'S EVE AND EPPIE'S CHILDHOOD

Molly Farren's revenge on Godfrey is to present their child to the Squire at his New Year's Eve party.

An opium addict, she collapses in the snow and dies near Silas's cottage. The child enters his cottage and Silas mistakes her hair for his returned gold. He finds the collapsed Molly and goes to fetch Dr Kimble from the party. Godfrey recognises his daughter in Silas's arms but keeps silent.

Eppie changes Silas's life and character. He regains trust in God and humanity through Eppie's personality and the interest of the admiring villagers.

CHAPTERS 16–18: GODFREY AND NANCY MARRY AND A THEFT IS FINALLY SOLVED

Godfrey marries Nancy but after sixteen years they are childless. He wants to adopt Eppie but Nancy believes adoption is wrong. Dunstan's body is discovered in the quarry with Silas's gold. Godfrey tells Nancy that Molly Farren was his wife and that Eppie is his daughter. Unexpectedly, Nancy forgives him and they agree to adopt Eppie. Neither considers Silas.

CHAPTER 19 – CONCLUSION: EPPIE'S CHOICE AND A WEDDING

Godfrey apologises to Silas for Dunstan's theft. He offers to adopt Eppie – who refuses. Godfrey reveals he is Eppie's birth father; twice more, supported by Nancy, he offers to adopt Eppie. Twice Silas tells Eppie to consider her future. She turns the offers down. She chooses to stay with Silas and marry Aaron Winthrop. Godfrey and Nancy accept Eppie's decision, although they are very upset, and decide not to make her true parentage public. At their wedding, paid for by Godfrey who does not attend, Mr Macey voices the feelings of everyone – Silas has won the respect and admiration of all through his own actions.

DID YOU KNOW?

Godfrey refers to Molly as being 'demonic' while he sees Nancy as his 'good angel'.

DETAILED SUMMARIES

CHAPTER 1 – Silas moves to Raveloe

❶ Silas was falsely accused of theft in his previous town.

❷ His accuser, William Dane, was the real culprit.

❸ Lots drawn by the religious sect he belonged to have sealed his fate.

❹ Silas lost his faith and moved to Raveloe to start a new life.

EXAMINER'S SECRET
Always read the entire examination paper before you start writing!

The first page of the novel takes us back to early-nineteenth-century England (c.1800–5) before the changes of the Industrial Revolution. We read descriptions of activities, people and ideas that were already old-fashioned in 1861 – when the book was first published.

The author's style in the opening is important. Think about how George Eliot creates the slow pace of time and allows us to see Raveloe and its surrounding countryside.

DID YOU KNOW?
Ravello is a beauty spot outside Amalfi in Italy. George Eliot was in the nearby Naples area when she decided to write *Silas Marner*. Is the name a mere coincidence?

Outsider

When the novel opens, Silas Marner, the novel's main character, has been living in Raveloe for fifteen years. Silas Marner lives and works as a weaver outside the village of Raveloe. His work as a weaver makes him different from the farming community. An important theme is introduced: that he is an outsider.

Raveloe is a remote village where everyone is suspicious of newcomers – especially when they do an unusual job like weaving and have an unfortunate appearance. Silas chooses to live alone and at a distance from people.

Jealousy

Silas lives alone because, fifteen years earlier, Silas was falsely accused of theft by his best friend, William Dane. Church money had been stolen from the house of a dying member of the strict Christian group, meeting in Lantern Yard, to which they both belonged.

William, a young weaver of about Silas's age, had become jealous of Silas for two reasons:

- He had feelings for Sarah – the servant to whom Silas was engaged.

- Silas is highly respected by other members of their religious group because of his good life and the fits he suffered which seemed to their simple minds to have some sort of religious significance.

William betrays Silas

In his cataleptic fits, Silas went rigid and into a kind of trance but remained upright. He had had one of these fits as he watched over a dying leader of the church. William, who should have watched later, had seized this chance to steal the money. He accused Silas of theft and later married Sarah himself. William had planted evidence against Silas in his room and managed to fix the drawing of lots which 'proved' Silas guilty and expelled him from the church.

DID YOU KNOW?

A cataleptic fit is a fit in which the sufferer goes rigid in a state of suspended animation.

Community

Silas then decided that God could not exist, and, after his move to Raveloe, he lives only for his work and the money it brings. The author tells us through a flashback that Silas was once very different. His earlier trusting and generous personality is contrasted with his present character. Silas's continued unfriendliness and his refusal to help others with herbal cures (apart from Sally Oates) combine to keep the superstitious villagers continually distant and afraid, despite Silas's growing wealth. The villagers' old-fashioned, superstitious beliefs have not yet been changed by new ideas and inventions. The villagers avoid or fear Silas for various reasons. Some of these are not of Silas's making, but result from Raveloe's isolated position.

A sense of community or belonging is a key idea in this book. Look at the early similarities between Silas and William Dane in their religious group. Think about the ways a real Christian should behave in these circumstances. Compare this with the community's treatment of Silas and you realise that the place he has escaped to is very similar in attitude to the place he escaped from!

CHECKPOINT 1

In what ways does Silas differ from the villagers?

CHECKPOINT 2

Who else is falsely accused in the novel?

CHAPTER 2 – Silas grows apart from the community

1. Silas lives as a miserly hermit.

2. He has no contact with organised religion.

3. He earns a reputation locally as a natural healer.

4. His sole enjoyment in life is counting the money he earns from weaving.

CHECKPOINT 3

How does Silas's past influence his life in Raveloe?

Raveloe is described: it is totally different from Lantern Yard. The simple, plain chapel and strict narrow beliefs of Silas's earlier life as an evangelical Christian in a northern town make Raveloe seem like a foreign country because its inhabitants are easy about religion and live in comfortable plenty.

Silas the miserly outsider

Losing his spiritual life is a disaster to Silas who copes by spending hours mechanically weaving. Alone, for over fifteen years, Silas has become obsessed with work and is a miser. He looks and behaves in an increasingly odd manner. His gold has become his hobby and has replaced friends. To avoid his painful memories, Silas works at his household tasks and at his weaving 'like a spinning insect' (p. 16). The weaving changes Silas's personality. His aim is now the acquisition of gold itself instead of what the money could buy. He now needs little money as he no longer gives to the church. He increasingly enjoys seeing and touching his gold, which he keeps in leather bags in the floor under his loom.

EXAMINER'S SECRET

Always write a brief plan before you write your exam essay. It will keep your answer on track.

Note the **irony** that Silas hides his gold. Because of the setting (c.1805) Silas does not expect to be robbed, yet he hides his gold – and is robbed! The villagers know each other so well that robbers are rare. To enjoy his loot, a robber would have to leave the village which is his whole world: 'a course as dark and dubious as a balloon journey' (p. 20).

After helping Sally Oates's heart problem, Silas's refusal of his herbal medicines to other villagers increases their suspicion and dislike. The author gives the villagers a collective voice as they discuss and hold general opinions. Silas came from 'an unknown region' (p. 7). Throughout the book, look for their opinions on events and individuals.

CHAPTER 3 – The problems of Squire Cass and his sons

 DID YOU KNOW?
The name 'Cass', may come from the Latin word 'casus', meaning 'chance'. Godfrey believes in the god of a 'Favourable Chance'(Ch 9, p. 73).

❶ Squire Cass is a feckless widower.

❷ Godfrey, the eldest son, suffers from an ill-advised secret marriage.

❸ His brother, Dunstan, is blackmailing him to support a wasteful lifestyle.

❹ Godfrey gives Dunstan his horse to sell in order to raise the hundred pounds that he owes his father.

 DID YOU KNOW?
The name 'Lammeter' may derive from 'meter', meaning 'a measure', suggesting that Nancy's family leave little to chance!

Squire Cass is the largest landowner in Raveloe, although others, like Mr Osgood, are nearly his equal. As food producers, the farmers gain from the high food prices caused by the Napoleonic wars. They enjoy the easier winter months, visiting each other and holding parties. The villagers approve of this lifestyle, if only because by custom they receive the leftovers. They disapprove, however, of the Squire's upbringing of his sons after the death of his wife, and of their resulting characters. They hope the oldest, Godfrey, will rescue his family by marrying Nancy Lammeter, the capable and attractive daughter of a greatly respected neighbouring farmer. They greatly dislike his second son, Dunstan, known as Dunsey.

The lifestyle of the idle rich

We meet members of the small landowner class, who are often called 'the gentry' because they either own or rent their farms. The title of 'Squire', already old-fashioned elsewhere, is given to Mr Cass because he owns the most land in Raveloe. Careful reading of Chapter 3 gives details of the characters and daily lives of Squire Cass and his two oldest sons. It also reveals village opinion on them. Class divisions are very important in this book.

The villagers consider Squire Cass a bad father, another key theme in the book. Their clear opinions on the two oldest sons come just before we judge them for ourselves.

Godfrey has problems in addition to the money. He loves and, off and on, has been openly courting Nancy Lammeter. However, his marriage to Molly, to whom he once had been passionately attracted, is a secret. Molly's lower social class would make her unacceptable to the proud Squire. In any case Godfrey has tired of her, her drunkenness, her drugs and her demands for money. Godfrey's situation allows Dunstan to blackmail him for money. We are told the reasons why Godfrey married Molly Farren whom he now increasingly hates. In contrast, he sees Nancy as the ideal wife he has lost through his own faults.

CHECKPOINT 4

What options seem to be available to Godfrey if he tells his father about Molly?

Fifteen years after Silas moved to Raveloe, we meet the Cass brothers quarrelling on a dark November afternoon in their uncomfortable home – both have been drinking. Godfrey demands the return of money belonging to his father, the rent from a man called Fowler. His father believes that Fowler has not paid the rent, and says that he will order Fowler's possessions to be seized. Godfrey had lent the money to Dunstan who now refuses to repay it. Dunsey threatens to have Godfrey disinherited by revealing his marriage to Molly Farren, once a pretty barmaid.

Godfrey becomes so desperate that he considers telling his father the truth. This would make the Squire throw out both his sons. However, after Godfrey has considered this possibility, he decides to take up Dunstan's offer to sell Wildfire, his horse and the only valuable thing he owns.

CHECKPOINT 5

How do the people of Raveloe view the Cass family?

EXAMINER'S SECRET

The examiners have read the novel so they don't need to be told the story. Refer to aspects of the plot – do not write it out in detail.

Godfrey is unable to attend the hunt on the following day because he plans to go to Mrs Osgood's birthday dance where he hopes to meet Nancy. He wishes also to avoid Batherley, where the hunt will meet, because Molly Farren lives there. Most reluctantly, he agrees Dunstan will go in his place and sell the horse.

Now take a break!

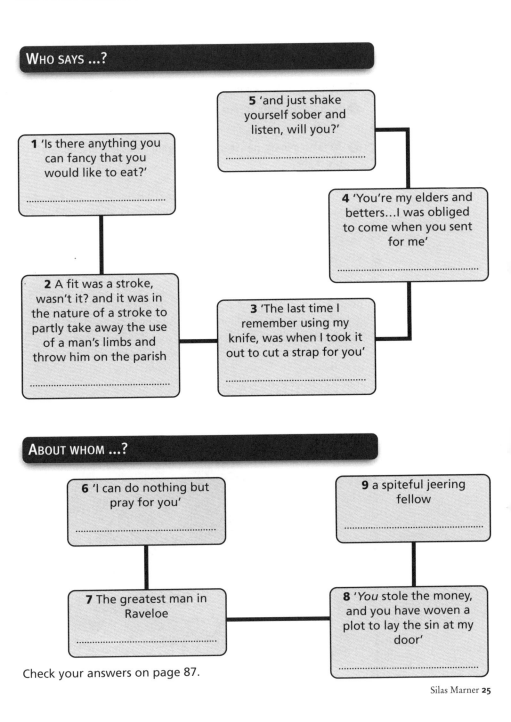

WHO SAYS ...?

5 'and just shake yourself sober and listen, will you?'

....

1 'Is there anything you can fancy that you would like to eat?'

....

4 'You're my elders and betters…I was obliged to come when you sent for me'

....

2 A fit was a stroke, wasn't it? and it was in the nature of a stroke to partly take away the use of a man's limbs and throw him on the parish

....

3 'The last time I remember using my knife, was when I took it out to cut a strap for you'

....

ABOUT WHOM ...?

6 'I can do nothing but pray for you'

....

9 a spiteful jeering fellow

....

7 The greatest man in Raveloe

....

8 'You stole the money, and you have woven a plot to lay the sin at my door'

....

Check your answers on page 87.

CHAPTER 4 – Godfrey's horse is accidentally killed

❶ Dunstan agrees a sale price for Godfrey's horse.

❷ He subsequently suffers a fall jumping a fence and the horse is killed.

❸ To raise money, he steals Silas's gold coins and disappears into the night.

As Dunstan rides past Silas's cottage to the hunt, he remembers the rumours about the weaver's gold. He believes Godfrey could persuade or frighten the old man into lending them enough money. He chooses, however, to enjoy selling Wildfire before explaining his plan to Godfrey. In this way, he hopes to upset Godfrey more.

A bargain is quickly made with Bryce who agrees to pay when the horse is delivered to Batherley stables. Then Dunstan decides on a day's hunting. Through Dunstan's careless riding, the horse falls at a hedge. It is pierced with a stake and dies. No-one sees the accident, and the uninjured Dunstan decides against hiring a horse in Batherley. He thinks again of Silas's gold. He decides he will force Godfrey to borrow it immediately. He is glad of the increasing mist and darkness which hide the shame and peculiarity of his having to walk.

CHECKPOINT 6

Why did Dunsey have the hunting accident?

Holding a whip makes him feel better, even though it is engraved with Godfrey's name. He is able to use it to feel his way. While he walks, he wonders how the weaver can be persuaded and bullied to lend his money. The sight of Silas's cottage lights makes him decide to act immediately himself.

Dunstan is surprised to find the cottage empty and unlocked. The door key is holding roasting pork in position near the fire. He wonders if Silas has fallen into the nearby quarry, the Stone-pit. He jumps to the conclusion that the weaver is perhaps dead. This idea makes Dunstan think no-one will realise the money is gone. He begins to hunt for it. Cottages having limited hiding places, he quickly finds the two leather bags holding the gold hidden beneath loose bricks near the loom. Suddenly frightened, Dunstan decides to hide in the darkness outside the cottage. There he can think about what to do with the bags.

CHECK THE BOOK

A way to examine the novel's broader perspective would be to compare and contrast it with a novel set in a different period and place, e.g. Harper Lee's *To Kill a Mockingbird* (Minerva, 1991) covers many of the issues raised in *Silas Marner*.

CHECKPOINT 7

What is the literary term given for when the weather is supposed to reflect a person's fortunes?

Dunstan's wickedness

The unpleasantness of Dunstan Cass is directly revealed to us through the events of the day when the hunt meets at Batherley. Dunstan's theft links Silas with Godfrey Cass, preparing us for their interweaving parallel plots.

Ironically Dunstan thinks Silas may have fallen to his death in the quarry. The bad weather and decreasing visibility prepare us for the death of Dunstan, an example of the **pathetic fallacy**.

George Eliot uses traditional images of light and dark to symbolise good and evil. A good example of this is Dunstan slipping into the darkness.

EXAMINER'S SECRET

Always use quotations to support your answers.

CHAPTER 5 – Silas tries to find the thief

❶ Silas discovers his gold has been stolen.

❷ He concludes the culprit is a local poacher.

❸ He rushes to the local inn for assistance.

Dunstan just misses Silas returning to enjoy his roast pork and his gold. Needing string for the next day, Silas had happily left his isolated cottage unlocked instead of delaying his dinner. He is so short-sighted that he notices nothing different in his cottage. Once warm again, he decides to enjoy looking at his gold as he eats his meal.

The discovery of the empty hole is a shock. He searches everywhere before again feeling the empty hole. Then he sinks into the seat of his loom – as in his previous trouble at Lantern Yard, Silas instinctively turns to his loom and works.

He considers the possibility of a thief. The pouring rain has destroyed any footsteps. Rather than believe cruel spirits are hurting him a second time, he decides the local poacher, Jem Rodney, must be the robber. He rushes off to the Rainbow pub where he expects to find men with the authority to help him. Mrs Osgood's dance has

CHECKPOINT 8

What is Silas's first reaction to his loss?

removed the most important villagers, but the rest make a larger than usual group in the pub kitchen.

Silas in trouble

Despite all his previous experience and his own antisocial behaviour since coming to Raveloe, Silas still has faith in humans because he rushes to the Rainbow for help.

Silas is as good as Dunsey is bad. His only concern is to regain his gold, not to hurt or punish anyone. Dunsey, however, had enjoyed the idea of frightening the old man.

CHAPTER 6 – A discussion at the Rainbow

1 At the Rainbow the locals are engaged in typical banter.

2 We learn of their narrow lifestyle and interests.

As a woman, George Eliot could never have been present in a village inn – making this description of the scene the more remarkable.

We meet Mr Snell, landlord of the Rainbow, his cousin Bob Lundy the butcher, Mr Dowlas the farrier, Mr Macey the tailor and parish clerk, Mr Tookey the tailor and deputy clerk, and Ben Winthrop the wheelwright. We hear how the villagers treated previous outsiders (see **Themes**) which can be contrasted with their treatment of Silas. The villagers' talk covers a slaughtered cow; the Lammeter family who have sold it; some unkind teasing and jokes about Mr Tookey; Mr Macey's well-known information on the Lammeters; a Lammeter–Osgood wedding; the previous owners of the Lammeters' rented farm and its possible ghost. A lively but unfinished argument on ghosts and fair bets ends the chapter.

George Eliot uses different forms of humour (see **Language and style**) which relieve the tension of Silas's loss. The trivial incidents seriously reported, the villagers' enjoyment of the retelling of well-known stories and their arguments paint a comic scene of rural life.

CHECKPOINT 9

What is the role of Mr Snell in this discussion?

EXAMINER'S SECRET

Keep your quotations short.

The narrowness of village life

We are introduced to the working men of the village enjoying their pipes, beer and leisurely conversation. They are described as a group and detailed information is given on individuals. The descriptions bring the characters to life, reflecting their separate personalities and showing village attitudes.

George Eliot here uses dialect and dialogue to bring us closer to the villagers and give us insight into their lives.

CHAPTER 7 – The villagers try to help Silas

1 Silas tell his story of the crime.

2 The poacher is cleared of guilt.

3 An investigation is set on foot.

CHECKPOINT 10

What object seemed to be the most important pointer towards the identity of the thief?

Each of the villagers thinks that Silas is a ghost until he begs for help. He seems mad when he accuses Jem Rodney of theft. Mr Snell makes him sit down to dry out. He orders him to tell his story. Convinced by Silas's distress, the men believe he has been robbed by the devil. Their proof of Jem's innocence makes Silas regret and apologise for his accusation. He remembers when he himself was falsely accused. Mr Dowlas suggests they inform the village constable, Mr Kench, who is ill. They decide they need to appoint a substitute constable and inspect the scene of the crime. After argument, Mr Snell, who is suggested as deputy constable, and Mr Dowlas go with Silas to Mr Kench.

A turning point in Silas's life

Silas appears like the ghosts the villagers have been discussing, at once changing the congenial atmosphere as they are shocked into reality.

This is a turning point – Silas has only wanted his gold, now he discovers the warmth of the village community as they listen to his story. In turn, because he is half-crazed by his genuine distress, their attitude changes and they react with caring concern.

CHAPTER 8 – Dunstan goes missing

❶ Godfrey knows that his marriage prevents him from winning the hand of the woman he really wants – Nancy Lammeter.

❷ He is concerned that the missing Dunstan is spending his money.

❸ Unable to find him, he resolves to reveal the truth of his situation to his father.

❹ The next day, he decides to talk to his father only about the missing money.

After Mrs Osgood's party, Godfrey Cass does not worry about the absence of Dunstan and Wildfire. He is too busy enjoying memories of Nancy and blaming himself for his secret marriage. Next day he focuses on Silas's loss. Suggestions about the possible identity of the thief are made and rejected before Mr Snell remembers a visiting pedlar. He connects this pedlar with a tinder box discovered near Silas's cottage. Other details about the robbery have to be discussed in the pub by the men. Silas gladly believes the pedlar was the thief but Godfrey does not agree.

Worried the missing Dunstan is spending his money, Godfrey rides off for news. He meets Bryce who tells him of the agreed sale and Wildfire's death. Believing the uninjured Dunstan will reappear to harm him, Godfrey eventually decides to tell his father everything on the next day.

He goes to bed having rehearsed how best to break the news. He fears his father's violent anger and his habit of refusing to change his decisions. Godfrey hopes his father's pride will prevent him disinheriting his son. However, in the morning, he wakes to his old fears of disgrace and losing Nancy. He decides to confess only about the money.

EXAMINER'S SECRET

Keep checking on the wording of the question you are answering. This will stop you from drifting off the subject.

Godfrey's character weakness

Godfrey's weak willpower is emphasised by his rehearsal of what he will tell his father. He decides to rely on luck to extricate him – a key part of his character.

He need not tell his father the whole truth. He prefers to rely on his 'old disposition to rely on chances which might prove favourable to him' (p. 67).

He concludes that he will attempt to 'soften his father's anger against Dunsey' (p. 67) and thereby not rock the boat too much!

Chapter 9 – Godfrey talks to his father

❶ Godfrey reveals to his father that he has given Dunstan money from a tenant.

❷ Squire Cass suspects Godfrey is being blackmailed but cannot find out why.

❸ He suggests that Godfrey should marry Nancy in order to restore the family fortunes.

❹ He instructs Godfrey to sell Dunstan's horse and ban him from the house.

 **EXAMINER'S SECRET**
The best candidates are able to cross-reference by showing connections between different parts of the novel: such as between Silas's rejection by the community in Lantern Yard and his eventual acceptance by the people of Raveloe.

At a late breakfast, Godfrey talks to his father. Squire Cass explains he is too poor to replace Wildfire who, he understands, is only injured. This misunderstanding makes Godfrey's confession about Fowler's rent even harder. The Squire threatens to throw out all his sons and to remarry. He guesses the absent Dunstan has blackmailed Godfrey to lie over a guilty secret.

Ignoring his own bad land management and his past refusals of Godfrey's help, the Squire blames his increasing money problems on his sons. He offers to ask Nancy Lammeter to marry Godfrey. He believes Nancy could make Godfrey's decisions for him, and help him reform.

DID YOU KNOW?

Nuneaton and Bedworth Borough Council have set up a George Eliot Fellowship to celebrate her achievements.

Squire Cass

Further information is given on the character of Squire Cass. He hopes the war will continue, keeping prices high. He feeds meat to his dogs, in contrast to the villagers' diet (Dolly Winthrop treats Silas to 'lard-cakes' in Chapter 10, p. 81). He never quite understands fully what is going on and this enables Godfrey to escape the full reality of his situation since his father will accept half-truths.

His attitude towards his sons suggests he is not quite the caring concerned father we might have expected. He is happy to let them carry on without any real discipline until he feels they are actually hurting him. Then he steps in and becomes a disciplinarian.

The Squire orders Godfrey to cancel the instructions against Fowler and orders instead the sale of Dunstan's horse. Pleased to have sorted the rent money, Godfrey worries that a possible chat between the Squire and Nancy's father might force him to refuse to marry her. Like most people with problems, Godfrey hopes luck will save him. The narrator warns us that most events are the results of actions we choose to do.

GLOSSARY

lard-cake a rich sweet cake made from bread dough

CHAPTER 10 – The villagers accept Silas at last

❶ **The search for the thief is unsuccessful.**

❷ **Silas loses the will to live.**

❸ **Mrs Winthrop tries to cheer him up.**

❹ **Silas spends Christmas Day alone.**

❺ **The Cass family have a family party though Dunstan is still missing.**

EXAMINER'S SECRET
Make sure you understand what is meant by terms such as 'evaluate', 'compare' and 'analyse' so that you know what you are required to do in an examination.

Justice Malam orders a lengthy search for the pedlar, which is unsuccessful. The Squire decides to refuse to have Dunstan home. Dunstan's continued absence upsets no-one. His disappearance is not linked to the robbery on the same day because of his respectable family and the mental effects on the villagers of the Christmas partying. Godfrey imagines him planning his troublemaking return.

The men of the village talk about the robbery in the Rainbow. Two rival opinions are strongly held by the villagers: either the pedlar or evil spirits have robbed Silas.

In his distress Silas moans softly at his work or by the fire at night. The villagers begin to pity him, deciding he is harmlessly crazy. We are introduced to Mrs Winthrop. The narrator tells us of her character and activities in the village before presenting us with her conversation with Silas. The villagers speak to him in the village and visit his cottage. Some give presents of food, in a vain attempt to cheer him up. Several visitors suggest various reasons why Silas should be neighbourly and attend church.

CHECKPOINT 11
What is Dolly's attitude to church worship?

Despite the advice of his neighbours, Silas spends Christmas day alone, while the villagers go to church and feast. The Cass family, including their relatives Dr and Mrs Kimble, enjoy a family party. They do not mention or miss the absent Dunstan.

The narrator looks forward to the greatest seasonal event, Squire Cass's annual New Year's Eve dance. This assembles everyone who is anyone, in either Raveloe or Tarley. It will last overnight, and contrasts starkly to Silas's lonely Christmas.

The author reminds us that Godfrey's problems remain unsolved. Dunstan's return and his father proposing for him are not Godfrey's only worries. He is still afraid he will be forced to refuse to marry Nancy because he is already married to Molly. Molly, meanwhile, is demanding money.

Godfrey's argument with himself, as the chapter ends, allows us into his mind. It shows us the conflict between what he ought to do and what he wants to do.

EXAMINER'S SECRET

The good candidate will mention the importance of money in this society. Both to the Casses and to Marner at this point. Of course money ceases to be important to Marner as his integration within the Raveloe community grows.

> ### The village warms to Silas
>
> The villagers' changed attitude to Silas continues: they now regard him as crazy and needing help and sympathy. They encourage him to come to church which like the Rainbow is an important focus of community life.
>
> Dolly's childlike religious faith and belief in Providence (God) is so simple as to be almost superstitious. For example, she puts the religious symbol 'I.H.S.' (p. 82) on her lard-cakes without understanding its meaning.
>
> Dolly makes Aaron sing a carol as she believes it will do Silas good and encourage him to go to church. He is as bewildered by the music and 'church' (p. 83) as she is by the word 'chapel' (p. 83).

GLOSSARY

I.H.S. the first three letters of the name of Jesus in Greek

Now take a break!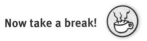

WHO SAYS ...?

1 'what's lacking to you? What's your business here'

....

5 'Two hundred and seventy-two pounds, twelve and sixpence, last night when I counted it'

....

2 'I'll pitch this can at your eye if you talk o'*my* stealing your money'

....

4 'Are you turning out a scamp? I tell you I won't have it'

....

3 'For it'll look bad when Justice Malam hears as respectable men like us had a information laid before 'em and took no steps'

....

ABOUT WHOM ...?

6 'what must you be letting him have my money for?'

....

9 enforced the doctrine by a present of pigs' pettitoes

....

10 'He came from a bit north'ard'

....

7 he was such a lucky fellow

....

8 'he's got a gift – he can sing a tune off straight, like a throstle'

....

Check your answers on page 87.

CHAPTER 11 – Squire Cass's New Year's Eve party

1 The Squire signals he wants Godfrey to marry Nancy.

2 Godfrey dances with Nancy.

3 Nancy does not discourage Godfrey's interest in her.

4 Godfrey resolves to enjoy the night despite the impossibility of his ever marrying her.

The discussion in the Rainbow (Chapter 6) revealed the individual personalities and attitudes of the village men; this chapter does the same for the higher social group in the village. There is a sense of community as the watching villagers comment and generally approve.

The lively description of the preparations for, and the events of, the party give much detailed information on the period: of travel; of fashion; of contrasting ideas on fashion and social position in town and country; of a country festival.

Nancy and her father, Mr Lammeter, are welcomed by Godfrey and Squire Cass when they arrive at the Red House for the New Year's Eve celebrations. Nancy greets Mrs Kimble, the Squire's sister who acts as hostess for him, before joining her Aunt Osgood and other ladies in the Blue Room changing for the dance. Her worries over her sister's journey are ended by Priscilla's arrival. The Miss Gunns watch Nancy dress and are offended by Priscilla's blunt speech. Priscilla Lammeter is an engaging contrast to Nancy and to the Miss Gunns with their town ideas. She is a practical, hard-working, blunt-speaking countrywoman. She chooses to remain unmarried, unusual for women at that time. George Eliot here draws attention to Nancy's country accent which would be used by all the villagers regardless of class. She mocks the town superiority of the Miss Gunns.

Nancy and Priscilla sit near the top of the table because they are important guests and Mr Crackenthorpe, the Rector, compliments Nancy's looks. Godfrey's noticeable silence annoys the Squire whose own comments publicly point to her as Godfrey's future wife.

EXAMINER'S SECRET
A reference to the possible derivation of Nancy's name would catch the examiner's eye.

CHECKPOINT 12

Why does Nancy consent to dance with Godfrey?

After amusing his female patients and teasing his wife, Dr Kimble asks Nancy for a dance. This makes the Squire force Godfrey into opening the first dance with her although she is unenthusiastic.

As Solomon Macey leads the procession from the parlour to the White Parlour for dancing, Mr Macey, Ben Winthrop and other privileged villagers watch and pass comments. They guess Godfrey and Nancy are a couple, though the real reason why these two leave the dance is that Nancy's damaged dress needs Priscilla's repairs. In the small parlour Nancy is deliberately cool to Godfrey until, carried away, he startles her into anger. This pleases him because it shows she still cares for him.

EXAMINER'S SECRET

Make your handwriting clear and legible.

CHAPTER 12 – Silas rediscovers gold

❶ Molly Farren is coming to reveal Godfrey's secret to his family.

❷ She collapses in the snow.

❸ Her child finds her way to Silas's cottage.

❹ He is unaware she has entered his cottage and finds her lying before his fire like a 'heap of gold' (p. 110).

❺ He retraces the child's footsteps and discovers the now-dead Molly.

EXAMINER'S SECRET

The examiner is looking for the good candidate to see the connection between Silas's lost gold and the new found gold of Eppie's curls.

While Godfrey talks to Nancy at the party, his wife, Molly Farren, is carrying their child towards Raveloe. She plans to reveal to the Squire she is Godfrey's secret wife and intends to arrive at the party in her rags. This will hurt Godfrey more. She has not used his money to buy food and clothes. Instead, she has bought opium to which she is addicted. Darkness falls as she walks, exhausted, along unfamiliar lanes. Craving her opium, she takes a dose before collapsing in the snow. She falls under a gorse bush.

As the unconscious Molly's arms lose their hold, her sleeping daughter wakes up. She toddles towards the light from Silas's open door. She reaches his fireplace where she falls asleep in the warmth.

Coincidences and parallels

George Eliot makes use of **coincidence** here: Molly collapses outside Silas's cottage, the door is open for the New Year's bells and Silas has a fit. The child is able to walk into his cottage at precisely the moment that Silas has a cataleptic fit.

Years before, Silas had loved and cared for his small sister. Since leaving Lantern Yard he has cared for no-one. Receiving care in his own distress from the villagers, here he is able to comfort and care for the child who is in even greater need. His return to being able to love has started.

Silas had begun looking out of his open door at nights. The villagers have told him to listen to the New Year bells which will bring him luck. Perhaps also his lost money will return. The door remains open while he has one of his fits. On recovering, he notices nothing changed inside his home.

EXAMINER'S SECRET
It is not a criticism of Eliot to mention that it is a real coincidence that Silas has a fit now. To do so is to indicate an important aspect of Eliot's technique.

CHECKPOINT 13
Why does Silas not see Eppie enter his house?

EXAMINER'S SECRET
There is no need to write reams. Two to three sides of an exam answer book offer enough space to gain top marks.

As he bends to mend the fire, he thinks he sees his returned gold on the floor. His poor eyesight prevents his seeing the fair-haired sleeping child. Touching the child, he thinks he is dreaming of his own small sister. The child seems to have been sent by Providence. He comforts and feeds her when she awakes crying for her mother. Her uncomfortable wet boots remind Silas that the child is real. He finds the footprints which lead to Molly's body half buried by snow.

CHAPTER 13 – Godfrey's fateful silence

❶ The party is interrupted by Silas carrying in Godfrey's child.

❷ Godfrey remains quiet.

❸ He denies knowledge of Molly.

❹ He now feels free to marry Nancy.

❺ Silas adopts the child as his own.

Squire Cass's party goes well and family, guests and servants watch Bob Cass dance; but Godfrey watches Nancy. Silas enters carrying the child whom Godfrey immediately recognises as his own. Silas asks Doctor Kimble to attend the dying or dead woman in the snow.

Godfrey Cass hopes his wife is dead. Godfrey guiltily decides not to identify Molly and his child as they would cost him Nancy. If Molly dies, he will be free to marry again. The child can be cared for and he will reform by marrying Nancy. Godfrey makes an excuse to see the dead woman. Sixteen years later he remembers every detail of his dead wife's face. He is pleased yet sorry that his daughter cannot recognise him.

Refusing Mrs Kimble's suggestion, Silas claims his right to keep the child. Godfrey feels better after giving him money for her keep.

Godfrey controls his feelings as he leaves with Dr Kimble. He is praised by Dolly Winthrop as he brings her to Silas's cottage. Dolly's praise of Godfrey is **ironic** – his motive is to make sure Molly is dead; it is not tender-hearted to disown his child. It is also ironical that sixteen years later he tries to regain his child.

Only the absent Dunstan can harm Godfrey who now decides secrecy is best for himself, Nancy and his child.

The guilty secret

The separate stories of Silas Marner and Godfrey Cass meet when Silas accepts the child and Godfrey rejects her. George Eliot stresses that Godfrey recognises his duty as father to the child through references to his mental struggle. Because he is selfish and weak, he prefers to try to marry Nancy and chooses to disown the child.

Godfrey's actions to those he should love, his wife and child, are in sharp contrast to Dolly's. She puts herself out for a stranger in need. Moreover, her husband and Mrs Snell can be relied on to help. This demonstrates the villagers' sense of community.

CHECKPOINT 14

What is Godfrey's 'evil terror' (p. 114) when he hears that Molly is dead?

 **EXAMINER'S SECRET**

A good answer picks out that Godfrey thinks that money is a substitute for love.

 EXAMINER'S SECRET

The rejection of his child must be the worst thing that Godfrey does.

CHAPTER 14 – Silas becomes a father

1 The villagers approve of Silas's selfless devotion to his new daughter, Eppie.

2 Silas is helped by Dolly Winthrop.

3 His life begins again as he is led into a 'calm and bright land… (by) a little child's' (p. 131) hand.

Molly Farren's apparently unimportant death permanently affects several lives.

Raveloe quickens its changing attitude to Silas because he adopts the orphan. They are interested in how he will cope. The women are generous with advice and warnings. Silas confides in and receives practical help and advice from Dolly Winthrop. She approves of his keeping the child.

Silas continues to link his loss of money with the child's arrival. He is determined to have all her love. Dolly asks Silas to have the child christened and to bring her to church.

Silas agrees, although he cannot connect Dolly's religion with his own past beliefs and experiences. She is surprised that Hephzibah (Eppie for short) is a biblical name.

Church attendance, together with Eppie's needs and interests, brings Silas into contact with the villagers. Silas discusses with Dolly how to punish Eppie but cannot bear to actually punish her. Together Silas and Eppie enjoy the countryside and Silas revives emotionally. The villagers and their children welcome Silas because of Eppie. His earnings become of little interest or value to him unless Eppie needs something. Silas accepts the villagers' advice. He is a changed man.

CHECKPOINT 15

Why does Dolly maintain that Eppie should be christened?

 DID YOU KNOW?

In the Bible the giving of a new name indicates that God is giving the person a new chance.

Silas finds a new life

On the title-page of the first edition, George Eliot quoted William Wordsworth about the effects following the arrival of a child. In this chapter Silas begins to change because of Eppie – this is an important theme.

The religion of the town chapel is very different from the established church. Silas does not understand Dolly's religion. He agrees to have Eppie christened and brings her to church because he wants to do everything helpful to her and live by Raveloe customs. Now he is choosing to join the village community.

 DID YOU KNOW?
The poetry of Wordsworth (1770–1850) was very influential in Eliot's thinking.

CHAPTER 15 – Godfrey loves his daughter

1 Godfrey cares for his daughter from afar.

2 Dunstan is still missing.

3 He is free to marry Nancy.

Godfrey Cass secretly watches Eppie grow and occasionally, as chance offers, gives small presents to Silas. No longer afraid of the absent Dunstan, he feels reformed and looks forward to marriage and a family with Nancy. Eppie will be provided for.

The irony of Godfrey's rejection of Eppie

Godfrey is relieved to have disowned Eppie. **Ironically**, the weak and selfish Godfrey is not the reformed man he believes himself to be. His gifts to Silas depend on chance and he promises to himself to help Eppie – in the future. His marriage will be built on a lie. Ironic also is his dream of playing with his children – he will be childless.

The chapter ends ironically – a 'father's duty' (p. 133) does not end with providing money for a child. The previous chapter details the hours of devoted love Silas puts into bringing up Eppie. The contrast between Silas and Godfrey is again highlighted.

 EXAMINER'S SECRET
Always finish a little early so that you can check what you have written!

Now take a break!

Test yourself (Chapters 11–15)

Who says ...?

1 'As I say, Mr Have-your-own-way is the best husband, and the only one I'd ever promise to obey'

....

5 'Let me give something towards finding it clothes'

....

4 'I think those have the least feeling that act wrong to begin with'

....

2 'Ha, Miss Priscilla, the sight of you revives the taste of that super-excellent pork-pie'

....

3 'It does make her look funny, though – partly like a short-necked bottle wi'a long quill in it'

....

About whom ...?

6 (her) mind resembled her aunt's to a degree that everybody said was surprising, considering the kinship was on Mr …'s side

....

10 He felt a reformed man, delivered from temptation

....

9 'she'll be *my* little un… She'll be nobody else's'

....

7 His spare but healthy person, and high-featured firm face, that looked as if it had never been flushed by excess

....

8 She needed comfort, and she knew but one comforter

....

Check your answers on page 87.

CHAPTER 16 – Time passes

1 Sixteen years have elapsed.

2 Godfrey and Nancy remain childless.

3 Silas has rediscovered his Christian faith through Eppie.

4 They note the lowered water-level in the Stone-pits.

5 Eppie wishes to marry Aaron Winthrop.

Sixteen years have changed the villagers. Squire Cass is dead. Mr and Mrs Godfrey Cass are described leaving Sunday church followed by Mr Lammeter and Priscilla.

Silas eventually has been able to discuss with Dolly the false accusation against him at Lantern Yard. They agree it was a test of his Christian faith, which he has regained through Eppie. Silas confides details about his past to Dolly, whose faith explains it as a test from God. The reasons are unimportant to humans. Silas has enough faith to accept this idea.

When Eppie joins Silas, she suggests a wall to protect the garden which will also include the gorse bush where her mother died. Silas has given Eppie her mother's wedding ring, and although Eppie often thinks of her mother 'She hardly thought at all of the father of whom it was the symbol' (p. 146). Demonstrating the stones nearby .which are available for the wall, she notices the newly lowered water level in the quarry. Silas explains that it results from drainage ordered by Mr Cass to improve the land he has acquired from Mr Osgood.

Eppie speaks to Silas about her marrying Aaron. The young man has suggested they should then all live together. Silas decides to consult Dolly. He points out to Eppie that one day she will need the care of a younger man to replace himself.

EXAMINER'S SECRET
The lowered water level is a clue the writer leaves for herself which she can later capitalise upon!

A happy home-life

Detailed description shows the physical and mental changes between Silas and Eppie and the Winthrops. We see their happy home life, and learn of the changes a child has made to Silas – a major theme.

Village opinion approves of the gifts and cottage improvements made by Mr Cass. Silas is greatly admired by the villagers, who feel he deserves his good luck. Eppie and Silas demonstrate their love by their tact and consideration for each other in discussing her marriage.

CHECKPOINT 16

Why does Silas tell Dolly about his past?

CHAPTER 17 – The family problems of Godfrey and Nancy

1 No living child has been born to Godfrey and Nancy.

2 Nancy has not agreed to their adopting Eppie despite Godfrey's obvious keenness.

3 A commotion in the village has detained Godfrey away from the house.

Nancy's changes to the Red House are described as Priscilla and Mr Lammeter prepare to leave after Sunday dinner. Priscilla approves of Godfrey's farming changes. Maybe a dairy will cheer Nancy who is upset by Godfrey's unhappiness at being childless.

Godfrey walks his land on Sunday afternoons while Nancy holds the Bible and thinks. Since their stillborn baby fourteen years before, she has twice refused Godfrey's wish to adopt Eppie. Nancy believes Providence intends them to be childless.

As Eppie's birth father, Godfrey believes adopting her will be easy. He fails to understand the love between Silas and Eppie and the hurt he will cause. He lists to himself the social advantages of adoption to Eppie. Because he does not know Silas, Godfrey thinks he will agree.

The servant arrives early with tea. She enjoys alarming Nancy over the villagers' unusual activity. Nancy is afraid and wishes Godfrey would return, fearing that he has come to harm in some way. **Ironically**, she is right but not in the way she had supposed.

Nancy is a good woman who loves her husband. Her personality is limited, as forecast in Chapter 11, by the rigidity of her methods and her narrow view of Providence. Her argument against adopting Eppie is based on hearsay of one case.

> **CHECKPOINT 17**
>
> What did Nancy feel was the greatest disappointment of her husband's life?

The price of Godfrey's silence

George Eliot reflects a moral tone as Godfrey begins to reap what he has sown.

Godfrey's unhappiness at being childless is increased by his secret knowledge that he alone is to blame. By disowning Eppie, he gave her to Silas. Unaware Godfrey is Eppie's father, Nancy's narrow religious views make her decide against adoption.

Nancy and Godfrey recognise good qualities in each other. Nancy feels she was right to refuse to adopt Eppie. Godfrey feels the truth about Eppie would kill Nancy's love for him even if it did not kill her. Their childless marriage seems his punishment for disowning Eppie.

 **EXAMINER'S SECRET**

The good candidate will notice how Eliot constructs a character whose behaviour we believe in and who helps to shape the story.

CHAPTER 18 – Ghosts of the past return

❶ Dunstan's skeleton has been found in the Stone-pit.

❷ The revelation has also solved the mystery of the theft of Silas's gold.

❸ Godfrey reveals to Nancy that Eppie is his child.

❹ Nancy is not shocked but insists that the injustice must now be put right.

❺ Godfrey resolves to confront Silas and claim Eppie as his own.

CHECKPOINT 18

What positively identified the skeleton as belonging to Dunstan?

Godfrey enters in shock, ending Nancy's relief at his return. He tells her of the discovery and identification of Dunstan's skeleton in the newly drained Stone-pit.

She is surprised at the strength of his reaction, until he tells her that Dunstan stole Silas's gold. It lies in the quarry beside the skeleton. Disgraced by Dunstan's theft, and at last determined to hide nothing, Godfrey tells Nancy the truth about his first wife. She learns that Eppie is his child.

Godfrey's excuse is that the truth would have lost him Nancy. Nancy feels she would have accepted Eppie as Godfrey's daughter. Their married life might have been very different. She tells Godfrey that Eppie has been wronged and nothing is worth committing injustice. Again Godfrey realises he is defeated by his own faults. He decides to approach Eppie that night, although Nancy warns him of difficulties.

EXAMINER'S SECRET

A high-quality response will identify that Godfrey is affected by his own failings as much as those of others.

Nancy's strength and Godfrey's weakness

Nancy's rigid beliefs benefit Godfrey – she does not leave him to return to her father as he fears. She sticks by him and agrees he must do his duty by Eppie.

In the previous chapter, Godfrey misjudged Silas; here he misjudges his wife who surprises him with her generous reaction.

Godfrey is unable to empathise with Silas and Eppie and how they will feel. Nancy has greater insight – she expects difficulties because of Eppie's age.

Chapter 18 continued

An important chapter

This very brief chapter is very important. The circumstances of Dunsey's death reveal a family disgrace: that he, the son of one of the leading families in the area, has stolen money from Silas Marner. Dunsey has paid for the crime with his life.

It forces Godfrey to confront the hidden disgrace in his own life. Belatedly he confesses to Nancy that he has 'lived with a secret on [his] mind' (p. 162), that of the true identity of Eppie.

Nancy's strength is seen in her response to the revelation. She weeps for the lost opportunity to have raised Eppie as their own daughter but significantly she has no desire to prolong the deception: Eppie and Silas must know and as soon as possible.

She will hide no skeletons in her life.

Now take a break!

Who says ...?

1 'for Mr Cass's been so good to us, and built us up the new end o' the cottage'

....

5 'When God Almighty wills it, our secrets are found out'

....

4 'it wouldn't do to leave out the furze bush'

....

2 'the Bible as you brought wi' you from that country – it's the same as what they've got at the church?'

....

3 'I know the way o' wives; they set one on to abuse their husbands, and then they turn round on one and praise 'em'

....

About whom ...?

6 The tall blond man of forty is not much changed

....

10 'Do you think I'd have refused to take her in, if I'd known she was yours?'

....

7 Had she really been right in the resistance which had cost her so much pain six years ago?

....

9 'We've found him – found his body...'

....

8 'She manages me and the farm too'

....

Check your answers on page 87.

CHAPTER 19 – The moment of truth

❶ Silas and Eppie are talking of their love for each other.

❷ Nancy and Godfrey arrive with their proposal about Eppie's future.

❸ Silas is shocked but wants Eppie to make her own choices.

❹ Eppie insists that her only father is Silas.

❺ Godfrey finally realises that his rejection of her as a child was an unforgivable error.

Later that night, Silas speaks of his misery and his need for the gold before Eppie's arrival. They speak of their love for each other. Silas explains that the returned gold is useful but he is free from its spell.

Mr and Mrs Cass arrive and Godfrey apologises for Dunstan's theft of Silas's gold. Eppie's garden provides Godfrey's excuse to talk about her future. Silas feels hurt and uneasy listening to Godfrey's plans. He invites Eppie to reply for herself. She refuses Godfrey's offer of adoption; she cannot leave the people she knows and loves. She is content and does not wish to be a lady.

Duty versus love

Silas is counting his blessings as Godfrey and Nancy arrive to claim Eppie. He is threatened with losing her, his new treasure, on the day his old treasure returns.

Nancy feels they are disturbing Silas and Eppie 'very late' (p. 166) – sixteen years late! Godfrey should have claimed Eppie as a baby. Godfrey will 'make a lady' (p. 168). Silas always feels uneasy when his 'betters' like Mr Cass are present.

Duty is insisted on by Godfrey (because it now, selfishly, pleases him) and Nancy tells Eppie that in law she owes it to Godfrey (something unpleasant she must do). Contrast their ideas of duty with Eppie's feelings about the people she has grown up with and loves.

DID YOU KNOW?

When the Casses discuss with Silas the future of Eppie there is gold on the table and there is the gold of Eppie's curls: it is a symbolic contest between the two!

Upset by the refusal of his plans, Godfrey's anger leads him to reveal Eppie's parentage. He cannot understand Silas's point of view.

As Godfrey and Silas argue, Godfrey masks his selfishness by talking about Eppie's gain. Silas replies truthfully from his heart although he is afraid of blocking her opportunities. Silas again invites Eppie to choose her future life, this time knowing her birth father. Nancy sympathises with Silas's position but, because of her social class and love for Godfrey, she believes her husband to be in the right.

Silas withdraws his objections and does not try to influence Eppie's choice. This makes Nancy and Godfrey think that she will agree to their offer. However, Eppie carefully explains her reasons for refusing. Nancy suggests Eppie should agree to Godfrey's wishes because he is her legal father. Eppie only recognises one father: Silas. She explains that she plans to continue living with him. She will care for him with the help of the man she has promised to marry. Godfrey had felt very noble about his decision to adopt Eppie. He considers his rejection of her as a baby to be the worst action of his life. Eppie's refusal means he is prevented from feeling good about her. Very upset, he quickly leaves the cottage. Nancy follows him after promising to visit again.

> **CHECKPOINT 19**
> What does Silas feel that Eppie might miss most of all if she declines Godfrey's offer?

 EXAMINER'S SECRET
Higher-level achievement begins at the point where you show you are aware that you are being marked!

CHAPTER 20 – The consequences of Eppie's choice

1 Nancy and Godfrey agree to keep secret his true relationship to Eppie.

2 Nancy is pleased that Eppie will marry Aaron.

3 She is sorry for her husband but feels that he deserved Eppie's rejection.

4 She encourages him to accept what has happened.

We return home with Nancy and Godfrey. They realise Eppie will never be their daughter. In the circumstances they agree to continue hiding that Godfrey is Eppie's birth father. He decides to reveal it in his will. He has had enough of hidden crimes like Dunstan's. Nancy is relieved that her relations will only know of Dunstan robbing Silas.

DID YOU KNOW?

When she stopped attending church as a teenager, George Eliot faced such uproar that she changed her name.

Godfrey guesses that Eppie will marry Aaron Winthrop. Nancy feels Aaron is a good choice because he is serious and hard-working. They discuss Eppie's character and her resemblance to Godfrey. He feels that his punishment for rejecting her is that she dislikes and will misjudge him. Nancy feels it is right that Godfrey suffers. She tries to cheer him up by telling him he has always been a good husband. She encourages him to try to accept what has happened and the position he is in.

Godfrey's character has at last grown as he realises that some wrongs cannot be put right and that money cannot solve everything.

He comments on the **irony** of his situation – he once wanted to appear to have no children, now he is forced to seem childless.

CHAPTER 21 – Silas returns to Lantern Yard

❶ Silas decides to revisit the scene of his former humiliation at Lantern Yard.

❷ He is unable to recognise anywhere except the jail where he had once been imprisoned.

❸ Where Lantern Yard stood, a factory has been built.

❹ He returns now to Raveloe, the place he can finally call home.

❺ He has regained his faith and a true family.

CHECKPOINT 20

Silas thinks he sees people coming out of chapel at midday. How is he mistaken?

The next day Silas tells Eppie that for some time he has wanted to revisit Lantern Yard. The return of his stolen gold makes such a visit possible. He wants to question the minister, Mr Paston, about the church money stolen so long ago. He also wants to tell him about religion as it is lived in Raveloe. For different reasons, both Eppie and Dolly think the visit a good idea.

At first Silas recognises nothing of the town where he worked. Industry has changed it enormously in thirty years. He becomes excited when he recognises the town jail and the streets near Lantern Yard. Eppie is increasingly uneasy and upset by the town's size, activities and ugliness.

They discover that for more than ten years a large factory has stood on the site of Lantern Yard. This so shocks and upsets Silas that Eppie is afraid he will have a fit. No-one is able to tell Silas what happened to the chapel, its minister and congregation.

Raveloe is now home to Silas. Dolly Winthrop comforts him when he tells her that the truth about the theft is lost forever. She points out that it remains true that Silas was wrongly accused. Maybe the supernatural powers wanted this to happen to him. It does not matter if she and he never understand the reasons for this. Silas agrees. Through Eppie, who has chosen to stay with him, he has recovered enough faith for the rest of his life.

EXAMINER'S SECRET

Read through your work when you have finished. If you have forgotten to put in paragraphs, the examiner will understand if you indicate in the margin where you want new paragraphs to begin.

Silas finally emerges from darkness

The rapid changes of the Industrial Revolution have completely transformed the town. Silas and Eppie are both appalled by the conditions and noise. Prison Street and the jail are images of the misery of factory workers' lives.

Light and dark are images of faith. The town is dark and the streets narrow. The narrow religion of Lantern Yard has disappeared – the light Silas once lived by. Dolly told Silas she would be glad of any light he could bring back from his visit and comfortingly accepts the truth is in the dark unknown when he returns. Silas realises he himself received light (or faith) when Eppie came. It will be enough, now she has promised to stay with him.

DID YOU KNOW?

George Eliot is buried at Highgate cemetery (East) in London, not far from Karl Marx.

CONCLUSION – The loose ends are tied up

❶ Eppie and Aaron are married.

❷ Godfrey has paid for the happy couple's reception but feels unable to attend the wedding itself.

❸ The villagers welcome the couple as full members of their community.

❹ They return to Silas's cottage which has been extended and improved by its owner, Mr Godfrey Cass.

Conclusion continued

Eppie and Aaron marry on a warm sunny day in early summer. Notice the weather again fits human feelings – early summer sun shines on Eppie, in the wedding dress of her dreams, marrying the man she loves.

Mrs Cass has given Eppie the wedding dress of her dreams. She walks home from church between Aaron and Silas. Dolly and Ben Winthrop follow them. Arriving with her father for a day with Nancy, Priscilla enjoys watching the wedding group. It is a shame that Godfrey has had to go for the day to Litherley. He will miss his present of a reception at the Rainbow. It is right that he has helped Silas whom Dunstan had hurt.

Priscilla feels Nancy would have been lucky to adopt a child like Eppie. She and her father agree they could enjoy a youngster. Priscilla's and Mr Lammeter's discussion revives the theme of a child's influence transforming lives. It is **ironic** that if Godfrey had been a true father, Nancy would have brought up the child.

DID YOU KNOW?

In her later years, George Eliot loved wearing fashionable hats, especially ones with enormous ostrich feathers!

Too disabled and old to go to the church or the reception, Mr Macey sits ready to give a speech to the passing wedding group. He reminds everyone that he was the first to stand up for Silas. He hopes the young couple will have good luck even though he could not take part in the service, and they have had to have Tookey instead.

Outside the Rainbow the villagers enjoy the time between the wedding and the meal. They respect Silas and agree he deserves good luck because of his treatment of Eppie. Ben Winthrop chooses to join his friends at the pub.

The other four go for a short interval back to Silas's cottage. His good landlord, Godfrey Cass, has extended and altered the cottage, and its large garden is complete. Eppie decides no-one could be happier or have a prettier home.

Justice is done!

Godfrey has generously provided the wedding feast but has absented himself for the day. It is Silas who appears as Eppie's father. The villagers feel Godfrey's action is right, considering the hurt Dunsey did to Silas. Ironically, Godfrey's secret wrong to Eppie was greater.

George Eliot ends the book with conventional happiness which reflects the moral code, that the good are rewarded while the evil are punished.

DID YOU KNOW?

George Eliot has her own fan club in Japan: The George Eliot Fellowship of Japan, founded in 1997.

Now take a break!

Who says ...?

1 'they'd have taken me to the workhouse, and there'd have been nobody to love me'

....

4 'I was the first to say you'd get your money back. And it's nothing but rightful as you should'

....

2 'You'd like to see her taken care of by those who can leave her well off, and make a lady of her'

....

3 'it seems as you'll never know the rights of it; but that doesn't hinder there *being* a rights'

....

About whom ...?

5 'he's very sober and industrious'

....

9 'he'd have nothing when I was gone'

....

10 a man (who) had deserved his good luck

....

6 always ill at ease when he was being spoken to by 'betters'

....

8 he had brought a blessing on himself by acting like a father to a lone motherless child

....

7 'had had the luck to find a child like that and bring her up'

....

Check your answers on page 88.

PART THREE

COMMENTARY

THEMES

Five main themes are discussed here – there are other issues and concerns which you can enjoy finding for yourself as you study the text.

EVERYDAY LIFE

During the book's thirty-year time span (1790–1820), George Eliot shows the great changes in daily life brought by the Industrial Revolution. Much of England's population shifted from rural agricultural to urban industrial society. By the end of the novel, she contrasts town conditions and attitudes (Chapter 21) to those of the country which are given throughout the book.

She recreates the period and its atmosphere through information and details on daily life provided by:

- Raveloe village and its area (Chapters 1, 2)

- Outsiders – newcomers or people different in any way (Chapters 1, 2)

- Housing (Chapters 1, 3, 4, 11, 12)

- The gentry (Chapters 3, 11)

- Festivals and celebrations (Chapters 11, 13)

- Attitudes – between the villagers and the gentry (Chapters 3, 9, 11, 13)

- The villagers (male) – work, interests and leisure (Chapter 6)

- Parenting (Chapters 3, 10, 14, 15, 19)

- Religion (Chapters 1, 10, 14)

- Superstition (Chapters 1, 6)

- Education and childcare (Chapter 14)

- Health and community care (Chapters 1, 11, 13)

? DID YOU KNOW?
An MP investigating factory conditions in Bradford, in 1833, described the children as 'all shapes of the letters of the alphabet': the effect of prolonged toil on their tender frames!

- Clothes and fashion (Chapters 6, 11, 22)

- Country activities, conditions, attitudes (throughout)

- Town conditions and attitudes (Chapters 1, 11, 21)

RELIGION

Young people, brought up by a deeply religious person or in a strongly religious environment, like the young Silas Marner and the young George Eliot, may not challenge their beliefs.

DID YOU KNOW?

Charles Darwin's *The Origin of Species* was published in 1859. It questioned the literal accuracy of the first chapters of Genesis.

The life and work of John Wesley (1703–91) had great appeal to poorly educated working people, especially those in towns. Small sects like the chapel congregation of Lantern Yard grew up in imitation of his followers who became known as Methodists because of their hardworking simple lives and orderly worship based on the Bible. They were also called evangelicals (after the New Testament writers) and non-conformists because they did not accept the established Church of England. They also rejected its organisational structure, believing that all Christians are equal and replacing priests by ministers.

In contrast, the established church continued in its traditional way, especially in country areas.

When thinking about the importance of religion in the novel, consider the following and find information on:

❶ The chapel in Lantern Yard (Chapters 1, 2, 10, 14, 21)

❷ The church in Raveloe (Chapters 2, 6, 10, 14, 16, 22)

For both the above, discover/think about:

- The beliefs held

- Its organisation; how it was run

- Its membership

- Attitudes to it

- Attitudes it encouraged

Consider the practical effects on peoples' lives from both chapel and church:

- On their beliefs

- On their attitudes to others

- On their actions

- On their lives

Perhaps George Eliot intended the reader to reach conclusions about how religion affected people both in the town and in the country.

DUTY

Duty was very important to the Victorian readers for whom George Eliot wrote. Those characters in the book who fail in their duty must be punished and those who do their duty must be rewarded. It is closely connected to a sense of justice and moral awareness. It involves our responsibilities to others and can come from our circumstances, from our beliefs, or both.

DID YOU KNOW?

There was no protection in Victorian England for those who lost their jobs – they went to the work-house.

In *Silas Marner* duty is presented through parenting and community. We have many examples of parents – natural and adoptive – if they do their duty their children turn out well; if neglected they turn out badly (except Eppie whom Silas adopts). Consider the parenting by the following, and the resulting children:

Parents	Child
Squire Cass (pp. 24, 68) – punished	Godfrey (p. 24) – weak, selfish
	Dunstan (p. 24) – vicious, evil
Godfrey (p. 172) – punished	Eppie (p. 118) – consider the result if she had gone, as would have been expected, to the workhouse
Dolly Winthrop and Ben (p. 48)	Aaron (p. 181) – model son
Mr Lammeter (pp. 25, 98) – rewarded	Priscilla (p. 152) – cares for her aged father
Silas (pp. 118, 129) – rewarded	Eppie (pp. 173, 183) – model daughter

In the same way the characters receive justice – the good (Silas) are
rewarded and the evil (Dunstan and Godfrey) are punished.

DID YOU KNOW?

In Victorian England, old or infirm people would be sent to the workhouse – unless helped by their children.

COMMUNITY

A sense of community is an important theme in the novel. It links
very closely with themes on people and environment, outsiders
and 'no man is an island': all human actions, open or secret, bring
results. Because the community at Lantern Yard wrongly accuse
Silas of theft and expel him (Ch. 1, p. 13), Silas comes to Raveloe
(Ch. 1, p. 7). He visits neither the church nor the pub (Ch. 1, p. 8)
where the community meet, and he refuses through his unfriendly
behaviour (Ch. 2, p. 19) to become part of the village. In turn, the
villagers' primitive sense of community makes them suspect and
fear newcomers like Silas (Ch. 2, p. 19), especially when he is so
different from them in so many ways.

A second theft (Ch. 4, p. 40), the loss of his gold, makes Silas seek
the help of the community (Ch. 5, p. 44) and the villagers support
him (Ch. 7, p. 59).

By adopting Eppie (Ch. 13, p. 118) Silas saves the community her
cost to the poor rate. This pleases and interests the community
(Ch. 14, p. 129). Eppie leads Silas into church and community
(Ch. 14, p. 130) – he is accepted and approved long before his
adopted daughter marries into the community (Conclusion, p. 181).

THE CONSEQUENCES OF A CHILD'S PRESENCE

This is another major theme and connects with parenting, duty and
community. A child has a ripple effect on the lives of the
surrounding people. This is recognised by Priscilla and Mr
Lammeter (Conclusion, p. 182) as they watch the returning wedding
group. Looking at Eppie, they both feel their age and miss the
interest in life and the hopes brought by children and young people.

At the beginning of the novel Silas seems older than his actual age of
around forty years (Ch. 2, p. 20). His lonely, miserly life brings him
no happiness (Ch. 2, p. 16). He works 'like the spider' (Ch. 2, p. 16)
without 'love and fellowship' (Ch. 2, p. 17). Like all weavers, his
figure 'shrank and bent' (Ch. 2, p. 20) through the weaving and the
weight of his 'heavy bag' (Ch. 1, p. 5).

As a result of Eppie's arrival, he is able to carry a much heavier load – Eppie and 'his yarn or linen at the same time' (Ch. 14, p. 129) and he goes 'strolling out' (Ch. 14, p. 126) with all the time in the world to enjoy nature and the countryside.

STRUCTURE

Silas Marner has been written in two parts: a larger Part One and a smaller Part Two.

The narrative covers two periods of time in Part One:

- c.1805 – opening fifteen years after Silas arrived in Raveloe which records events from mid November into the New Year

- c.1790 – a flashback to show Silas's experiences in Lantern Yard

A third period of time is covered in Part Two:

- c.1821 – a timeshift to go forward to events sixteen years after the opening

The plot of a book looks at patterns and connections between characters and events. As the book's plot presents the events of Silas's life, it also reveals

- His early character and attitudes to him

- The causes of events which affect or change him

- His final character and attitudes to him

Throughout the book, George Eliot balances the plot structure through people and events. Look for the balance from

- Mysterious appearances and mysterious disappearances

- Thefts and false accusations

- Examples of men/fathers and examples of women/mothers

- Types of religion and types of communities

 DID YOU KNOW?
When Nancy separated from her father to pin her hopes on Godfrey, she was about the same age as George Eliot was when she separated from her father.

- Examples of family life

- Town and country

In spite of the subtitle *The Weaver of Raveloe*, there is a second plot – the life of Godfrey Cass – which runs parallel to the story of Silas.

CHARACTERS

SILAS

Silas Marner, the skilled hand loom linen-weaver, of 'exemplary life and ardent faith' (Ch. 1, p. 9), is the hero of George Eliot's novel. His trusting personality is basically good and attractive (Ch. 1, p. 9) although his circumstances temporarily change him into an antisocial miser (Ch. 1, p. 14). His simple religious faith was lived out through his hardworking and self-denying life. Both were much admired (Ch. 1, p. 9) by the narrow-minded evangelical sect to which he belonged and generously contributed most of his earnings (Ch. 2, p. 17). Even his cataleptic fits made him 'evidently a brother selected for a peculiar discipline' (Ch. 1, p. 10).

Naive
Vulnerable
Temporarily an 'outsider'
Hardworking
Honest
Essentially loving

His naive faith is so strong and sincere that his betrayal, by his friend William Dane and by God failing to clear him, results in his total loss of faith in people and God. His personality dramatically changes (Ch. 1, p. 14).

EXAMINER'S SECRET

If you are asked to compare two characters, you need to show the ways they are similar as well as the ways in which they differ.

He moves to a rural community whose suspicions and fears he increases by inviting 'no comer to step across his door-sill' (Ch. 1, p. 7). He also never 'drinks a pint at the Rainbow' nor enjoys 'gossip at the wheelwright's' (Ch. 1, p. 8). He replaces friends by his obsession for his gold, for which he compulsively weaves. He remains in this numbed mechanical phase until circumstances again cause him to change. The theft of his gold makes him so desperate that he turns to the villagers for their help. They generously respond and feel he is more crazy than dangerous. Their advice and visits recognise his need.

'It's come to me' (Ch. 13, p. 115), the mysterious arrival of the child seems almost supernatural to Silas. Impulsively he decides 'I've a right to keep it' (Ch. 13, p. 115) and eventually, through the child, his life transforms a second time. In fact, his goodness, and other good qualities, had gone dormant and are reawakened through Eppie.

Through Eppie, he gains the friendship of Dolly Winthrop. In Dolly's wisdom and religious faith he finds peace over the false accusation of long ago, and regains his own faith in God (Ch. 21, p. 180). Through what he does for Eppie and the change she brings to his personality, he becomes an admired and respected member of the village community (Conclusion, p. 182). He has earned his good luck, his enlarged and improved cottage, his returned gold and his happiness in living with and being cared for by his beloved daughter and her husband (Conclusion, p. 183).

EPPIE

Eppie is an idealised character. She is a pretty two-year-old with golden hair and blue eyes contrasting with her dirty, shabby clothes when she toddles into Silas's cottage. Aged three, she has a 'fine capacity for mischief' (Ch. 14, p. 126) and loves the world and Silas (Ch. 14, p. 130). She is important to both the plot and Silas's character – she is the means by which Silas recovers emotionally and becomes part of the village community. Her character though remains relatively flat (see **Style**) and undeveloped.

Sixteen years later, as an attractive and neat 'blond dimpled girl of eighteen' with 'curly auburn hair' (Ch. 16, p. 138), she has a lively personality and is loving, generous and considerate of others. She is a good housekeeper in the happy home where she devotedly cares for her ageing father (Ch. 16, p. 149). She sensitively wishes to marry using her dead mother's ring (Ch. 16, p. 148). She is grateful to Silas for saving her from the workhouse and for his love and care (Ch. 19, p. 166).

She has shy good manners to Nancy and Godfrey (Ch. 19, p. 166), but shortly afterwards (Ch. 19, p. 169) her shyness has gone when she declines their offer because of her love for Silas and the villagers. She is unmaterialistic and without social ambition (Ch. 19, p. 169). Her shocked reaction on learning Godfrey is her father turns to repulsion (Ch. 19, p. 171). She speaks with cold decision (Ch. 19, p. 172) when she chooses Silas and remains faithful to her upbringing and friends (Ch. 19, p. 173). Although excited and wanting to score off Aaron by visiting the town (Ch. 21, p. 177), its reality shocks and horrifies her, and she cannot wait to be home (Ch. 21, p. 178).

Loving
Caring
Lively
Sensitive
Loyal
Joyful

GLOSSARY

ardent fierce

peculiar discipline (destined for a) special role in the church

Kindly
Weak
Selfish
Deceitful
Insensitive
Opportunist

GODFREY

Godfrey Cass is **ironically** described as 'fine, open-faced, good natured' by the approving villagers (Ch. 3, p. 24) when he already has much to hide. He goes through life acting on impulses and hoping luck will save him from the results of his actions. In this way he has secretly married Molly Farren and fathered a child, been blackmailed to embezzle money due to his father – and yet still somehow hopes to wriggle out of everything and marry Nancy Lammeter! We are told he has an easy disposition and prefers good. For a while fortune favours him: Molly dies, Silas takes Eppie and Nancy agrees to marry him. With all his privileges and his loving wife, in the end Godfrey is unhappy because, ironically, he has to appear childless, his only child apparently having died. He had a child whom he disowned – he did not deserve to be a father. Silas adopted the child and was truly a father to her.

Godfrey often seems to expect that money will solve his problems; he gives Molly money which she spends on opium; he gives Silas money when he adopts Eppie; he expects Silas and Eppie to agree to his adoption plans because of money, and finally, he pays for the wedding reception at the Rainbow.

The discovery of Dunstan's remains is a turning point in Godfrey's character when he admits 'When God Almighty wills it our secrets are found out' (Ch. 18, p. 162). He tells Nancy every fact that he had hidden from her, about Molly being his wife and Eppie his daughter, only to realise 'he had not measured this wife with whom he had lived so long' (Ch. 18, p. 163). Her surprising reaction makes him realise 'his error was not simply futile, but had defeated its own end' (Ch. 18, p. 163). His brief satisfaction when Nancy agrees to adopt Eppie turns to punishment when Eppie says 'can't feel as I've got any father but one' (Ch. 19, p. 173) and 'I should have no delight i' life any more if I was forced to go away from my father' (Ch. 19, p. 172) i.e. Silas. At last Godfrey admits 'There's debts we can't pay like money debts … Marner was in the right' (Ch. 20, p. 174). He recognises the irony of wanting 'to pass for childless once, Nancy – I shall pass for childless now against my wish' (Ch. 20, p. 174).

DUNSTAN

Dunstan (nicknamed Dunsey) is all bad. He drinks, gambles and enjoys making other people unhappy. The villagers have a low opinion of him: 'a spiteful jeering fellow' (Ch. 3, p. 24). He lies 'independent of utility' (Ch. 4, p. 35).

There is a suggestion that he tempted Godfrey into marrying Molly as 'the means of gratifying at once his jealous hate and his cupidity' (Ch. 3, p. 31). Perhaps he is jealous of Godfrey: 'You're my elders and betters, you know; I was obliged to come when you sent for me' (Ch. 3, p. 25). He borrows and spends money recklessly. He blackmails his brother into 'borrowing' money from their father. He is overconfident – he believes he is lucky because 'whenever I fall, I'm warranted to land on my legs' (Ch. 3, p. 30). He treats animals badly, killing Godfrey's horse Wildfire through his careless riding (Ch. 4, p. 35). He has a sadistic streak – he enjoys the idea of forcing Silas to lend his money (Ch. 4, p. 34). Walking home, he seizes the chance to steal the money hidden inside the empty cottage (Ch. 4, p. 38). When he disappears, people feel 'It was no matter what became of Dunsey' (Ch. 3, p. 24). It is the discovery of his body that forces Godfrey into telling Nancy the secrets of his past.

Selfish
No morals
Vicious
Evil
Bitter
Spiteful

DOLLY

Dolly is a 'comfortable' woman, 'good-looking, fresh-complexioned', with 'lips always slightly screwed' and a 'grave' expression (Ch. 10, p. 80). Her physical looks are unimportant, in contrast to Nancy with her care of external appearances.

Like Nancy, she is widely admired as a good woman and excellent housewife, but Dolly 'was the person always first thought of in Raveloe when there was an illness or death' (Ch. 10, p. 80). Unable to read, but practical and competent, she contentedly and sincerely lives 'her simple Raveloe theology' (Ch. 10, p. 84).

Very poor, she prefers 'a bit o' bread' (Ch. 10, p. 81) to the lard-cakes which she gives to Silas. The cakes, and later the baby clothes 'patched and darned, but clean and neat' (Ch. 14, p. 121), are examples of her sensitive generosity.

Motherly
Practical
Competent
Uncomplicated
Strong Christian faith
Non-judgemental

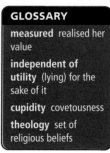

GLOSSARY

measured realised her value

independent of utility (lying) for the sake of it

cupidity covetousness

theology set of religious beliefs

Dolly's continued support 'without any show of bustling instruction' (Ch. 14, p. 120) and 'with a woman's tender tact' (Ch. 14, p. 122) turns her into Silas's valued friend as she enables him to rear her goddaughter, Eppie. Through her insistence that Silas 'take (Eppie) to church, and let her learn her catechise' (Ch. 14, p. 123), Silas regains his religious faith as he becomes accepted, then admired by the villagers (Conclusion, p. 182).

NANCY

The character of Nancy develops through the complimentary details of her looks and reflects her shallow concern over appearances. Admired by everyone, she is 'beautiful', 'thoroughly bewitching' (Ch. 11, p. 89), 'small and light' (Ch. 11, p. 90), and 'dainty and neat' (Ch. 11, p. 92). She is an outstanding and hardworking housewife (Ch. 11, p. 92).

Morally good

Excellent house-keeper

Model wife

Mentally strict and narrow

Becomes humbler and forgiving

She loves her family and although minimally educated, with a broad local accent, she has 'the essential attributes of a lady' (Ch. 11, p. 93). She loves Godfrey and understands her 'best of husbands' (Ch. 17, p. 153).

Most importantly for the plot, Nancy is 'slightly proud and exacting' (Ch. 11, p. 93) and rarely changes her mind. Her strict moral standards make her decide to refuse Godfrey (whom she loves) unless he reforms (Ch. 11, p. 96).

Later, Nancy's looks and appearance reveal some personality growth. Her 'beauty has a heightened interest' (Ch. 16, p. 137) and her 'firm yet placid mouth, the clear veracious glance' result from 'a nature that has been tested and kept its highest qualities' (Ch. 16, p. 137). Her clothes still have 'dainty neatness and purity' (Ch. 16, p. 137) and in her home 'all is polish' (Ch. 17, p. 151).

Her unchanged moral code makes her narrow and limited when she believes their baby's death and childlessness are 'Heaven's sending' (Ch. 17, p. 156), making her selfishly refuse Godfrey's pleas to try and adopt Eppie (Ch. 17, p. 156).

Her pride makes her feel characteristic shame (Ch. 18, p. 162) over Dunstan's crime but we admire her surprising lack of anger (Ch. 18, p. 163) and generous support when Godfrey confesses (Ch. 18, p. 164).

She is humble enough to believe she was not 'worth doing wrong for' (Ch. 18, p. 163).

IN TOWN

At Lantern Yard

William Dane is needed as a contrast to Silas and an example of the arrogant, confident person who could result from the narrow, exclusive group to which he belonged. He is able to betray Silas because he is as wicked as Silas is honest and trusting.

Sarah, Silas's betrothed, does not love him because her shallow affection allows her to follow public opinion against him and 'in little more than a month' (Ch. 1, p. 14) to marry William.

At Batherley

Molly Farren, a former barmaid, first wife of Godfrey Cass and Eppie's mother, creates suspense before she dies in the snow through her plan to expose her husband to his proud father. Addicted to opium, love for her child prevents her quietening its hungry cries with the drug which she bought with Godfrey's money instead of food and clothes. She represents the life some women endured in the towns of the period, for which she blames Godfrey rather than herself.

IN THE COUNTRY

Raveloe villagers

The vividly described and highly individual villagers provide us with humour and reveal the village hierarchy and tensions.

Mr Snell is the landlord of the Rainbow public house, the classless heart of social life for the men of the village. He was always very careful never to take sides (Ch. 6, p. 46), even when pushed by Mr Dowlas, the argumentative farrier (Ch. 6, p. 47). He acts as prompter to old Mr Macey (Ch. 7, p. 57) to take him through his repertoire of well-known stories. He is practical and comforting to the distraught Silas (Ch. 7, p. 55), tells the angry Jem to be quiet (Ch. 7, p. 56) and calmly refutes Silas's accusation of Jem (Ch. 8, p. 57). A leader of the villagers, he is keen to be deputy constable and amuses us when he most obligingly 'gradually recovered a vivid impression' (Ch. 18, p. 61) of the pedlar!

red haired. Also mild and 'I'm for peace' (Ch. 5, p. 41), he is a slow countryman. He needs time to think about answers and has music in his soul.

DID YOU KNOW?

Nancy has to keep her love for Godfrey a secret, just at the same age in her life as George Eliot was keeping secret her love for a married man.

GLOSSARY

show of bustling instruction bossiness

catechise understand the principles of Christianity

attributes qualities

veracious honest

Mr Dowlas, the opinionated and impulsive farrier, just has to be right – always! He is aggressive, able to become angry over nothing and uses 'bitter sarcasm' (Ch. 6, p. 53). He is the 'negative spirit' and proud of it.

Ben Winthrop is another much admired leader of village opinion. An 'excellent wheelwright', he reveals village interest and pride in its music and its 'piquant' sense of humour through the 'unflinching frankness' of his insults to Mr Tookey, who cannot sing (Ch. 6, p. 48). He is another example of parenting – devotedly proud of Aaron who 'sings like a throstle'.

CHECK THE NET

To find out more about George Eliot, type her name or 'Silas Marner' into your search engine such as Google and see where it takes you!

Aaron Winthrop is a good example of a flat character (see **Style**) who remains undeveloped. He is necessary as the 'perfect young man' who will bring the 'happy ending' by marrying Eppie.

Jem Rodney as the mole catcher is ideally placed to be the local poacher – his breaking the law is socially accepted and not in the same class as William Dane and Dunstan harming Silas. He informed the other villagers of Silas's fits, increasing suspicion of him. He causes Silas to remember the pain of an unjust accusation.

Raveloe gentry

Squire Cass is 'A tall stout man of sixty' with a 'slack and feeble mouth' and a 'hard glare', Squire Cass has an appearance of 'habitual neglect', and so has his house (Ch. 9, p. 68). He is an inconsistent man who fails to take action when he should and then blames everyone else. He is a hard landlord, who allows Fowler to get behind with his rent and is prepared to seize his possessions. He enjoys his position in the village, 'condescending' to visit the Rainbow (Ch. 3, p. 24), and 'patronising' his guests at New Year when he makes a great show (Ch. 11, p. 97). The easy-going villagers disapprove that 'he had kept all his sons at home in idleness' (Ch. 3, p. 24) and his sons fear his pride will disinherit them both (Ch. 3, p. 26) over money and Godfrey's secret marriage. He is an example of a bad father – he neglects his sons and then becomes angry at their actions.

In striking contrast, *Mr Lammeter* is greatly admired by the villagers as a gentleman (Ch. 6, p. 49), a father, and a farmer famous for the 'red Durham o' this countryside' (Ch. 6, p. 46). He brought up his daughters 'that they never suffered a pinch of salt to be wasted yet everybody ... had of the best' (Ch. 3, p. 25). He was a 'grave and orderly senior' (Ch. 11, p. 98) who would not allow his daughter to marry Godfrey before 'alteration in several ways'. He was lean and healthy, his face 'had never been flushed by excess' unlike Squire Cass whom he contrasts as a father.

DID YOU KNOW?
William Gladstone abolished tax in paper in 1861, thereby making the purchase of *Silas Marner* much cheaper!

Priscilla Lammeter is a 'cheerful looking lady' (Ch. 11, p. 93). 'That excellent housewife' (Ch. 5, p. 41) who generously gave Silas pork, her affection for her younger sister makes her agree to wear a dress which makes her 'yallow' (Ch. 11, p. 93). Cheerfully blunt about her looks: 'I am ugly ... the pretty uns do for fly-catchers – they keep the men off us' – she offends the Miss Gunns (Ch. 11, p. 94) without noticing. She has no wish to marry and is an unusual example of a single, practical, competent woman whose 'father's a sober man and likely to live' so 'the business needn't be broken up' (Ch. 11, p. 94). If you did not known that George Eliot was a woman, her creation of Priscilla might give you a real clue that she was!

Mr Crackenthorpe the Rector was 'not in the least lofty or aristocratic' (Ch. 11, p. 96). He was a 'merry-eyed, small featured grey haired man' with an impressive cravat who paid Nancy complements and joined in the dancing 'as part of the fitness of things' (Ch. 11, p. 102). 'The parson naturally set an example in these social duties' (Ch. 11, p. 102).

Mrs Crackenthorpe the Rector's wife (Ch. 11, p. 97) was a 'small blinking woman' who fidgeted with 'her lace, ribbons and gold chain' and made noises 'like a guinea pig'. The comical description continues when little Aaron wonders how does 'that big cock's-feather stick in Mrs Crackenthorpe's yead?' (Ch. 11, p. 103).

Doctor Kimble had followed the family tradition in becoming an apothecary. He lived very comfortably keeping 'an extravagant table' (Ch. 11, p. 98) and employing an apprentice (Ch. 13, p. 115). He is brother-in-law to Squire Cass, whose sister he married; they are childless (Ch. 13, p. 118). He has lent money to his nephew

GLOSSARY
red Durham a breed of cow originally bred in Durham
yead head

Godfrey in the past. A 'thin and agile man', he is generally lively and agreeable, except when playing cards.

Mrs Kimble enjoys 'a double dignity' (Ch. 11, p. 90) in the village as the doctor's wife and the Squire's sister. She is very fat but has 'much good humour' (Ch. 11, p. 98) and considers her husband 'clever and amusing' (Ch. 11, p. 100).

DID YOU KNOW?

Barbara Bodichon started a petition in 1866 for votes for women. In February 1918, Female householders aged over 30 were finally granted the vote.

Mr Osgood farms at The Orchards where he entertains generously (Ch. 3, p. 24) and his family have lived as long as the villagers can remember (Ch. 3, p. 23). His dead sister had been the wife of Squire Cass and mother of his four sons. Mr Osgood has a son, Gilbert.

Mrs Osgood is elderly, rather prim, with 'curls of smooth grey hair' (Ch. 11, p. 91). 'Devoted attachment and mutual admiration' (Ch. 11, p. 92) exists between her and her niece by marriage, Nancy Lammeter, although she disapproves of her niece Priscilla who was 'too rough' (Ch. 11, p. 93). She is another of the excellent housewives in the village (Ch. 3, p. 24).

LANGUAGE AND STYLE

GEORGE ELIOT'S NARRATIVE STYLE

Of all aspects of literature, the hardest to grasp is the writer's use of language and style. Writers are always faced with choice when they are telling a story. They choose what aspects of a narrative they will recount and they choose the words in which the story is told. *Silas Marner* is written in such a way that we, the reader, have a constant overview of what is happening. A story told by a single person allows us to enter that person's mind but gives a narrow view of what is going on.

In one chapter we can be watching Silas as he discovers the theft of his money; in the next we can be sitting in the Rainbow waiting for him to burst through the door with the awful news. This puts the reader in a godlike position, able to survey a wide range of lives all at once. It also creates some dramatic interest as we can see what is about to happen at times. Nevertheless, we are aware that George Eliot chooses for us what we shall see, as happens when Dunsey stumbles off into the darkness after stealing Silas's gold but when we are not told his fate at that time.

This lofty position we readers occupy enables us to compare different lifestyles and different ways of conducting one's life. We are also able to compare reactions to situations and form a judgement. After Eppie rejects Godfrey's offer to come 'home' with him, we are able to see the reaction of both Godfrey and Silas as the events are discussed. Moreover, we can judge from the reactions what George Eliot feels to be right and wrong.

The advantages of omniscient narration are:

DID YOU KNOW?
Telling the story through different eyes is known as omniscient narration.

● We are given an overview of society enabling us to draw conclusions by comparison.

● We are able to sympathise with different characters who are suffering as we can see through their unpleasantness.

At times we may feel as if George Eliot is playing with our feelings. Some chapters follow on from each other, taking us to the next stage in the narrative. She will, however, build in excitement by unexpected juxtapositioning of different events. At the end of Chapter 11, we have the New Year's Eve party in full swing and Godfrey on the point of moving closer to his beloved Nancy.

Eliot notes that he has a 'reckless determination to get as much of this joy...tonight' (Ch. 11, p. 106). At that precise moment though we suddenly realise his world is about to fall around his ears. The next chapter transports us to the 'snow-covered Raveloe lanes' (Ch. 12, p. 107) where Godfrey's wife is stumbling along carrying their child in her arms towards the unwitting Godfrey! It is the sort of narrative technique that makes compulsive reading.

CHECK THE BOOK
The Dictionary of Literary Terms by Martin Gray is an excellent guide to aspects of language use.

LANGUAGE IN THE NOVEL

We may also safely assume that Eliot was aware that she was writing for an educated readership, such is the difficulty of the language. Look at the reason given for Godfrey's ill-advised marriage to Molly: 'A movement of compunction, helped by those small indefinable influences which every personal relation exerts on a pliant nature, had urged him ito a secret marriage, which was a blight on his life' (Ch. 3, p. 31).

In other words, he married her because he felt sorry for her but there are some extra nuances of meaning within this that delicacies of expression are able to convey. Godfrey presumably had a 'pliant nature' which suggests a weakness in his character and Molly may have brought some emotional pressure to bear on him, one of the 'small indefinable influences' that George Eliot suggests changes lives.

TECHNIQUES OF STORY-TELLING

One of Eliot's tricks is the use of **coincidence**. On the one hand, this might be seen as a weakness in a story-teller for coincidences offer easy ways to propel a story. On the other hand, real life has far more coincidences and unlikely events than any writer would ever dare use so we may just as well accept them as unexpected developments in a narrative.

The series of coincidences surrounding the events on the New Year's Eve (see Chapters 12 and 13) is quite remarkable: Molly collapses outside Silas's cottage (p. 108); Silas has a fit at his open door, rendering him unconscious to the arrival of Eppie (p. 109); Eppie enters (p. 109); Molly dies (p. 117); and Silas decides to keep Eppie (p. 118).

EXAMINER'S SECRET

It is not a criticism of Eliot to mention that it is a real coincidence that Silas has a fit when Eppie first enters his house. To do so is to indicate an important aspect of Eliot's technique.

The use of **contrast** is quite common in literature. You have only to look at the mixture of the terrifying and the comic in Shakespeare to see how effective it can be, for the comic makes the terrifying even more frightening and vice versa. Eliot uses the technique often: between people (Silas and Godfrey, Ch. 19, pp. 168–9); between actions (Silas and Godfrey, Ch. 13, p. 118); between places or scenes (Raveloe Ch. 1, p. 7 and Lantern Yard Ch, 1, p. 15) and between atmospheres (town Ch. 21, p. 178 and country Conclusion, p. 181).

Novelists tend not to overdo the use of **dialogue**. Speeches between characters slow down the story, so writers use dialogue to do a variety of things such as reveal feelings in the way that relations between Godfrey and Dunstan are brought out in their quarrel (Ch. 3, p. 25). Dialogue also provides opportunities for humour or introducing local colour. The lengthy conversation in the Rainbow (Ch. 6, p. 46) offers a little light relief amid a grim sequence of events whilst also revealing the period of the book, the speech patterns and accents of the villagers. The style of conversation forms a contrast to that of the gentry (Ch. 11, p. 93) as well as a contrast to present-day speech.

IMAGERY

A very difficult aspect of literary study is the figurative language used by a writer. Figurative expression enables the writer to draw comparisons for his reader. In this way the reader brings his or her own experience into an understanding of the novel. **Images** and **symbols** are used frequently. Silas in his unthinking industry is described as 'a spider' (Ch. 2, p. 16) and a 'spinning insect' (Ch. 2, p. 17). Gold is his payment (Ch. 2, pp. 17, 21) and Eppie's hair is like gold (Ch, 12, p. 110, Conclusion, p. 181), thus forming in the reader's mind a certain link between the two in Silas's attitude. Light is an important symbol throughout: we have, for instance, Lantern Yard (note the **ironic** name) which stands for faith, while darkness – as in the blackness of night (Ch. 2, p. 16) – represents loss of faith and despair.

IRONY

The style of narration means that the reader knows more about what is really going on than the characters. We are able to see how they are likely to go wrong before they know themselves. This is **irony**. It is widely used in *Silas Marner* to great effect since Eliot is keen to let us see how people err when they do not know the whole story. For example, the narrator tells us the villagers' opinion of Godfrey (Ch. 3, p. 24) which is ironic since we know he has some rather unpleasant secrets. Similarly, it is **dramatic irony** that the reader knows that Godfrey has a child (Ch. 12, p. 107) but Nancy does not (Ch. 18, p. 162).

THE PATHETIC FALLACY

Pathetic fallacy is a belief that nature acts in sympathy with human actions. When something happy is occurring, the sun will be shining, and when terrible deeds are afoot, we may expect great storms. It is, of course, a mistaken belief though one we may often feel ourselves. It is worth noting that weather which responds to our emotions actually makes them that much more significant. The storm on the night Silas is robbed (Ch. 5, p. 44) helps to make the theft that much more of an offence against nature and, by contrast, the lovely weather at Eppie's wedding (Conclusion, p. 181) when 'the sunshine fell more warmly than usual' reinforces the sense that heaven is smiling down upon this union.

DID YOU KNOW?
The term 'pathetic fallacy' was invented by John Ruskin in a book he wrote in 1856.

RESOURCES

HOW TO USE QUOTATIONS

One of the secrets of success in writing essays is the way you use quotations. There are five basic principles:

1 Put inverted commas at the beginning and end of the quotation.

2 Write the quotation exactly as it appears in the original.

3 Do not use a quotation that repeats what you have just written.

4 Use the quotation so that it fits into your sentence.

5 Keep the quotation as short as possible.

Quotations should be used to develop the line of thought in your essays. Your comment should not duplicate what is in your quotation. For example:

> The narrator tells us that the story of the linen-weaver, Silas Marner, begins in the early years of the nineteenth century through the quotation 'in the early years of this century' (Ch. 1, p. 6).

Far more effective is to write:

> The narrator tells us that Silas Marner's story begins 'in the early years of this century' (Ch 1, p. 6).

However, the most sophisticated way of using the writer's words is to embed them into your sentence:

> The narrator reveals a linen-weaver named Silas Marner, worked at his vocation in the backward-looking village of Raveloe 'quite an hour's journey on horseback from any turnpike' (Ch. 1, p. 7).

When you use quotations in this way, you are demonstrating the ability to use text as evidence to support your ideas - not simply including words from the original to prove you have read it.

COURSEWORK ESSAY

Set aside an hour or so at the start of your work to plan what you have to do.

EXAMINER'S SECRET
Examiners **never** take marks away.

❯ List all the points you feel are needed to cover the task. Collect page references of information and quotations that will support what you have to say. A helpful tool is the highlighter pen: this saves painstaking copying and enables you to target precisely what you want to use.

● Focus on what you consider to be the main points of the essay. Try to sum up your argument in a single sentence, which could be the closing sentence of your essay. Depending on the essay title, it could be a statement about a character: The theft of his gold could have made Silas Marner more bitter and isolated. Instead he accepts responsibility for Eppie and becomes a happier person, accepted and admired by the Raveloe community; an opinion about setting: I think Raveloe represents a threatened community in a changing world. George Eliot believed country values were lost through the economic and social changes brought by the Industrial Revolution and world events; or a judgement on a theme: I think justice is the main theme in Silas Marner because, in the end, the characters who choose to do good are rewarded but those who neglect their duty or choose to do ill are punished.

EXAMINER'S SECRET
If you are asked to make a comparison, use comparing words such as, 'on the other hand', 'however' and 'by contrast'.

● Make a short essay plan. Use the first paragraph to introduce the argument you wish to make. In the following paragraphs develop this argument with details, examples and other possible points of view. Sum up your argument in the last paragraph. Check you have answered the question.

● Write the essay, remembering all the time the central point you are making.

● On completion, go back over what you have written to eliminate careless errors and improve expression. Read it aloud to yourself, or, if you are feeling more confident, to a relative or friend.

If you can, try to type your essay, using a word processor. This will allow you to correct and improve your writing without spoiling its appearance.

SITTING THE EXAMINATION

EXAMINER'S SECRET
Beware of feeling you have to finish an answer because you have reached the bottom of the page.

Examination papers are carefully designed to give you the opportunity to do your best. Follow these handy hints for exam success:

BEFORE YOU START

- Make sure you know the subject of the examination so that you are properly prepared and equipped.

- You need to be comfortable and free from distractions. Inform the invigilator if anything is off-putting, e.g. a shaky desk.

- Read the instructions, or rubric, on the front of the examination paper. You should know by now what you have to do but check to reassure yourself.

- Observe the time allocation – and follow it carefully. If they recommend 60 minutes for Question 1 and 30 minutes for Question 2, it is because Question 1 carries twice as many marks.

- Consider the mark allocation. You should write a longer response for 4 marks than for 2 marks.

WRITING YOUR RESPONSES

- Use the questions to structure your response, e.g. question: 'The endings of X's poems are always particularly significant. Explain their importance with reference to two poems.' The first part of your answer will describe the ending of the first poem; the second part will look at the ending of the second poem; the third part will be an explanation of the significance of the two endings.

- Write a brief draft outline of your response.

- A typical 30-minute examination essay is probably between 400 and 600 words in length.

- Keep your writing legible and easy to read, using paragraphs to show the structure of your answers.

- Spend a couple of minutes afterwards quickly checking for obvious errors.

WHEN YOU HAVE FINISHED

- Don't be downhearted – if you found the examination difficult, it is probably because you really worked at the questions. Let's face it, they are not meant to be easy!

- Don't pay too much attention to what your friends have to say about the paper. Everyone's experience is different and no two people ever give the same answers.

EXAMINER'S SECRET

Always have a spare pen!

IMPROVE YOUR GRADE

Your potential grades in any examination can always be improved. Every candidate everywhere starts at the same point: a blank answer booklet. An examiner marks your work according to a mark scheme that is applied to all candidates and no examiner knows in advance your level of achievement.

You must realise that the examination board has determined that your answer book contains more than enough space for any candidate to get the highest marks so there's no need to rush your writing in order to fill up three or four extra sheets!

EXAMINER'S SECRET

Keep an eye on the clock so you do not run out of time.

Moreover, the examination board knows that the two hours your examination is scheduled to last is enough for any candidate to secure the highest marks **without rushing**. You are not expected to write solidly for two hours since the examiner confidently believes that you will spend at least some of the time thinking!

So take your time. Think carefully, plan carefully, write carefully and check carefully. A relaxed performer always works best – in any field and in every examination!

Whatever you are studying, the way to be completely at ease with it in an examination is to know it inside out. There is no substitute for reading and re-reading the text.

Let's consider how you could approach the following question:

What part does gold play in the lives of Godfrey Cass and Silas Marner?

- To begin with you might want to define what you, mean by 'gold' since in the novel it represents both money and the golden curls of Eppie.

- You might then move on to looking at the debt that Godfrey finds himself in with his father, and the way he is manipulated by his brother, Dunsey.

- Next consider the way Silas becomes obsessed with his gold and the effect the theft of it has upon him.

EXAMINER'S SECRET

A short quotation is always more effective than a lengthy one.

- The arrival of Eppie at Silas's house would make a good sequel to this for her golden curls are seen in some way as a replacement for what he has lost.

- You might conclude by showing how Silas prefers the gold of the curls to money, whilst Godfrey still thinks money is the answer to everything.

IMPROVING YOUR RESPONSE FROM A D TO A C

- Instead of writing that Godfrey is angry with his brother because he has not repaid the loan, you would write that Godfrey's anger over the debt had shown itself in the way that 'he had been drinking more than was good for him' (Ch. 3, p. 26).

- Instead of writing an account of the argument between Godfrey and Dunsey, concentrate on the importance of money to Godfrey, that he is so upset that he threatens Dunsey that he will 'knock [him] down' (Ch. 3, p. 26).

- Instead of noting that Godfrey is desperate for a solution, illustrate it by observing that he even allows Dunsey to take his horse for sale because he has 'got nothing else to trust to' (Ch. 3, p. 29).

IMPROVING YOUR RESPONSE FROM A C TO A B

- Instead of writing that Silas regarded the gold he hoarded as being his sole purpose for living, you could note Eliot's comment that the guineas lie on the table as he eats his meal and for him the guineas 'were a golden wine' (Ch. 5, p. 43).

- Use detail from the whole chapter that collectively creates a sense of the desolation Silas feels when he loses his money: his hands and knees are 'trembling' (Ch. 5, p. 43); he emits a 'cry of desolation' (Ch. 5, p. 44); he feels 'he must go and proclaim his loss' (Ch. 5, p. 44) to the locals.

- Instead of commenting that the writer creates the impression that Silas is obsessed with his gold, you could indicate the ways in which gold was important to him to the point of being an obsession: that his interest in gold amounted to a 'worship', that he 'had clung with all his force of his nature to his work and his money' (Ch. 5, p. 42), and that the soul-destroying work he did served only to create a 'monotonous craving for its monotonous response' (Ch. 5, p. 42), i.e. work equalled money.

CHECK THE FILM
You can increase your understanding and enjoyment of *Silas Marner* through dramatisations such as the BBC video version (2001), starring Ben Kingsley.

IMPROVING YOUR RESPONSE FROM A B TO AN A

- Instead of just observing that Godfrey and Silas have different feelings towards what is right for Eppie, you could suggest that for Godfrey the important thing for a father was to ensure that 'it [Eppie] was well provided for. That was a father's duty' (Ch. 15, p, 133). Silas on the other hand regards her as a 'blessing' (Ch. 19, p. 166), one without whom he says he would 'think [he] was forsaken again' (Ch. 19, p. 166).

- You could identify the central image of gold and its close association with Eppie. In Chapter 19, Silas and Eppie are sat at the table on which lies the recovered gold. He tells her he fears she might be lost to him again, 'changed into the gold' (p. 165), and that he thinks that would be 'a curse come again, if it had drove you from me' (p. 165). Ironically exactly that choice is about to present itself as Godfrey effectively attempts to buy Eppie back.

- Instead of just pointing out that Godfrey and Silas have a different attitude towards money, you could also examine the differences in their backgrounds. It is quite clear that the Casses are an establishment family whose influence and lifestyle depend entirely upon inherited money. The very worst fate that can befall a man is to be disinherited, as the Squire shows when he delivers the harshest punishment on Dunsey. For Silas, money is a 'symbol of earthly good, and the immediate object of toil' (Ch. 2, p. 17). Money does not drop into your lap – you have to work for it!

- Instead of just observing the techniques used by the writer, you could also consider the moral purpose of the novel. Two stories are intertwined in the novel, one about a man who has suffered in a previous existence and whose desperate poverty does not prevent him from giving everything to a child, the other about a man who has abused his privileged position. The first man is enriched by love, the second man feels that money alone will solve the problems. Godfrey's final words do not suggest a man plunged into misery by his failure, rather a philosophical acceptance that he cannot have everything: '...it *is* too late to mend some things...' (Ch. 20, p. 176). For Silas there is a final guarantee of lasting happiness as Eppie looks around their house and declares, 'I think nobody could be happier than we are' (Conclusion, p. 183).

SAMPLE ESSAY PLAN

EXAMINER'S SECRET
Always write a plan for every answer. The biggest failing of candidates is not sticking to the question.

A typical essay question on Silas Marner is followed by a sample essay plan in note form. This does not present the only answer to the question, merely one answer. Do not be afraid to include your own ideas and leave out some of the ones in this sample! Remember that quotations are essential to prove and illustrate the points you make.

In your opinion who made the best father: Squire Cass, his son Godfrey, or Silas Marner? How did George Eliot influence your choice?

PART 1

Introduce your subject by explaining what you would look for in a good father. For example, his personality, circumstances, what he says and does, his motives, the opinions other characters have of him and his relationship with his child or children.

PART 2

Develop the subject by considering each of the fathers: compare and contrast them. Remember to include supporting evidence through short quotations, ideally only two or three words long, whenever possible. Identify the skills George Eliot used to reveal her characters and how this influences your choice. You could use:

- **Description** – the personality of each character and appearance if relevant

- Use of **narrator's voice** and any other use of language features

- Use of **coincidence;** other features of plot

- Use of **irony**

- Use of **contrast**

- Use of **symbols** or **imagery**

- Use of **atmosphere**

Explain your understanding of George Eliot's purpose in using these skills.

PART 3

Conclude by measuring each character against your list for an ideal father. Name and explain your choice of best, second best, and worst father.

FURTHER QUESTIONS

❶ The good are rewarded and the bad are punished – is *Silas Marner* a moral tale?

❷ Compare and contrast two novels of your own choice, one from the nineteenth and one from the twentieth centuries. Use your understanding of the social, historical and cultural backgrounds of each to explain which you enjoyed most.

❸ What part do injustice and misunderstanding play in the life of Silas Marner?

❹ After reading the text of *Silas Marner* and watching the video, which version do you prefer? Explain your reasons for your choice. (To do this essay, you need to be aware of all changes and differences from the original text and their effects.)

❺ Compare the success of George Eliot with that of another author (like Harper Lee) in making a man face and solve his problems. Think about the effects on their writing of where and when the authors lived.

EXAMINER'S SECRET
The best candidates know the set books thoroughly and have formed a point of view about them? What do you think *Silas Marner* is about?

EXAMINER'S SECRET

Don't waste time looking to see how your friends are doing!

6 Compare the characters of three of the women in the novel. What effect does each have on Silas?

7 Coincidences – how important are they in the novel?

8 Did reading the novel make you change your mind? What do you now feel about the author's presentation of people and events?

9 Write entries from Nancy's diary which cover:
- Her meeting with Godfrey at the New Year's ball
- Their failure to have children
- The visit to Silas and Eppie

10 How would the book be changed if Eppie had agreed to return home with Godfrey?

Now take a break!

allusion a reference which briefly recalls something in another text

atmosphere mood – varies according to what is said or done

character the imaginary people in a book, also their personalities as revealed by descriptions of what they say and do – or by what others say about them

coincidence artificial unrealistic organisation of time and place of events to suit plot

context events before and after an incident in the book

contrast when opposites are introduced to balance or highlight characters, places, events or issues

description using words to create scenes, objects, people, behaviour, attitudes and atmosphere

dialect the special words and style of speaking particular to an area or region

dialogue speech and conversation used by the book's characters

dramatic irony when the plot allows the readers of a book to know more than some of the characters in the book

imagery means use of metaphors and similes; also means use of objects to rouse feelings

irony speaking or writing one thing while really meaning another. It includes sarcasm

metaphor the writer states that one thing is another. There is no intention to deceive and it is intended to arouse the imagination

narrator's voice this is not the personal opinion of the author, but a mechanism or mask used to tell the story. Can be first person, speaking through 'I' or 'we'. Can be third person, refers to 'he', 'she', 'they' etc.

pathetic fallacy when a writer emphasises a character's mood by linking it to the surrounding world. This is often done through nature and natural events such as weather, but can be man-made

personification to give human qualities to an animal or object

plot organisation of the events in a book

sarcasm an ironic speech which mocks, taunts or insults the person spoken to; but amuses onlookers

setting time (period) and place where the events of the novel take place. Can be used to reveal characters and atmospheres

simile figure of speech which compares unlikely objects or people through shared characteristics: uses 'like' or 'as'

symbol one thing is used to represent another

CHECKPOINT HINTS/ANSWERS

CHECKPOINT 1 He is a loner who comes from a different part of the country. He does not attend church. He is uninterested in using his skill as a herbalist to help the villagers.

CHECKPOINT 2 Silas himself falsely accuses Jem Rodney of stealing his gold (Chapter 7).

CHECKPOINT 3 Silas keeps himself to himself; he does not attend church; he spends his life working his loom; he becomes a miser.

CHECKPOINT 4 He either becomes a soldier or commits suicide!

CHECKPOINT 5 The squire is regarded with some respect as the head of the community though he is held to be a bad father. Godfrey is seen as a generally worthy son while Dunstan is known as a ne'er-do-well.

CHECKPOINT 6 He fancies riding to the hunt and after a drink of brandy becomes over-confident.

CHECKPOINT 7 The **pathetic fallacy**.

CHECKPOINT 8 He gives a 'ringing scream, the cry of desolation' (Ch. 5, p. 44).

CHECKPOINT 9 As the landlord of the pub, Mr Snell directs the conversation.

CHECKPOINT 10 A tinder-box was discovered half-sunk in a ditch some way from the village which may have been carried by a travelling pedlar a month before.

CHECKPOINT 11 She attends church regularly: the prayers and the hymns make her 'feel so set up and comfortable' (Ch. 10, p. 83).

CHECKPOINT 12 She is not especially keen on him, as he will find out, but she does not want to be rude to him.

CHECKPOINT 13 At this crucial point in the story he has a cataleptic fit.

CHECKPOINT 14 Eliot says that in his 'kindly disposition' (Ch. 13, p. 114) there was an ugly inmate: the fear that Molly 'might *not* be dead' (Ch. 13, p. 114).

CHECKPOINT 15 Eppie like all children is 'helpless'. Christening is one way that an adult parent can ensure she will be saved from harm.

CHECKPOINT 16 He has learned through being accepted by her that he can trust someone at last, and finds it easy to open his mind to her.

CHECKPOINT 17 She thought that he was unable to get used to the idea that they had no children.

CHECKPOINT 18 Godfrey identifies the hunting-whip with his name on it that he knew Dunstan had the day he went away.

CHECKPOINT 19 He says that she will have chosen to live among poor folks when she might have had 'everything o' the best' (Ch. 19, p. 172).

CHECKPOINT 20 They are, in fact, men and women coming from a factory 'for their mid-day meal' (Ch. 21, p. 179).

TEST YOURSELF (CHAPTERS 1–3)

1 The narrator (*Chapter 1*)

2 Mr Macey (*Chapter 1*)

3 Silas Marner (*Chapter 1*)

4 Dunstan Cass (*Chapter 3*)

5 Godfrey Cass (*Chapter 3*)

6 Silas Marner (*Chapter 1*)

7 Squire Cass (*Chapter 3*)

8 William Dane (*Chapter 1*)

9 Dunstan Cass (*Chapter 3*)

TEST YOURSELF (CHAPTERS 4–10)

1 Mr Snell (*Chapter 7*)

2 Jem Rodney (*Chapter 7*)

3 Mr Dowlas (*Chapter 7*)

4 Squire Cass (*Chapter 9*)

5 Silas Marner (*Chapter 7*)

6 Dunstan Cass (*Chapter 9*)

7 Dunstan Cass (*Chapter 4*)

9 Aaron Winthrop (*Chapter 6*)

8 Mr Crackenthorpe (*Chapter 10*)

10 Mr Lammeter's father (*Chapter 6*)

TEST YOURSELF (CHAPTERS 11–15)

1 Priscilla Lammeter (*Chapter 11*)

2 Doctor Kimble (*Chapter 11*)

3 Ben Winthrop (*Chapter 11*)

4 Nancy Lammeter (*Chapter 11*)

5 Godfrey Cass (*Chapter 13*)

6 Nancy Lammeter (*Chapter 11*)

7 Mr Lammeter (*Chapter 11*)

8 Molly Farren (*Chapter 12*)

9 Eppie (*Chapter 14*)

10 Godfrey Cass (*Chapter 15*)

TEST YOURSELF (CHAPTERS 16–18)

1 Silas Marner (*Chapter 16*)

2 Dolly Winthrop (*Chapter 16*)

3 Priscilla Lammeter (*Chapter 17*)

4 Silas Marner (*Chapter 16*)

5 Godfrey Cass (*Chapter 18*)

6 Godfrey Cass (*Chapter 16*)

7 Nancy Lammeter (*Chapter 17*)

8 Mr Lammeter's daughter, Priscilla (*Chapter 17*)

9 Dunstan Cass (*Chapter 18*)

10 Nancy talking about Eppie (*Chapter 18*)

TEST YOURSELF
(CHAPTERS 19–CONCLUSION)

1 Eppie (*Chapter 19*)

2 Godfrey Cass (*Chapter 19*)

3 Dolly Winthrop (*Chapter 21*)

4 Mr Macey (*Conclusion*)

5 Aaron Winthrop (*Chapter 20*)

6 Silas Marner (*Chapter 19*)

7 Nancy Lammeter (*Conclusion*)

8 Silas Marner (*Conclusion*)

9 Eppie talking about Silas (*Chapter 19*)

10 Silas Marner (*Conclusion*)

NOTES

NOTES

Maya Angelou
I Know Why the Caged Bird Sings

Jane Austen
Pride and Prejudice

Alan Ayckbourn
Absent Friends

Elizabeth Barrett Browning
Selected Poems

Robert Bolt
A Man for All Seasons

Harold Brighouse
Hobson's Choice

Charlotte Brontë
Jane Eyre

Emily Brontë
Wuthering Heights

Shelagh Delaney
A Taste of Honey

Charles Dickens
David Copperfield
Great Expectations
Hard Times
Oliver Twist

Roddy Doyle
Paddy Clarke Ha Ha Ha

George Eliot
Silas Marner
The Mill on the Floss

Anne Frank
The Diary of a Young Girl

William Golding
Lord of the Flies

Oliver Goldsmith
She Stoops to Conquer

Willis Hall
The Long and the Short and the Tall

Thomas Hardy
Far from the Madding Crowd

The Mayor of Casterbridge
Tess of the d'Urbervilles
The Withered Arm and other Wessex Tales

L.P. Hartley
The Go-Between

Seamus Heaney
Selected Poems

Susan Hill
I'm the King of the Castle

Barry Hines
A Kestrel for a Knave

Louise Lawrence
Children of the Dust

Harper Lee
To Kill a Mockingbird

Laurie Lee
Cider with Rosie

Arthur Miller
The Crucible
A View from the Bridge

Robert O'Brien
Z for Zachariah

Frank O'Connor
My Oedipus Complex and Other Stories

George Orwell
Animal Farm

J.B. Priestley
An Inspector Calls
When We Are Married

Willy Russell
Educating Rita
Our Day Out

J.D. Salinger
The Catcher in the Rye

William Shakespeare
Henry IV Part I
Henry V
Julius Caesar
Macbeth

The Merchant of Venice
A Midsummer Night's Dream
Much Ado About Nothing
Romeo and Juliet
The Tempest
Twelfth Night

George Bernard Shaw
Pygmalion

Mary Shelley
Frankenstein

R.C. Sherriff
Journey's End

Rukshana Smith
Salt on the snow

John Steinbeck
Of Mice and Men

Robert Louis Stevenson
Dr Jekyll and Mr Hyde

Jonathan Swift
Gulliver's Travels

Robert Swindells
Daz 4 Zoe

Mildred D. Taylor
Roll of Thunder, Hear My Cry

Mark Twain
Huckleberry Finn

James Watson
Talking in Whispers

Edith Wharton
Ethan Frome

William Wordsworth
Selected Poems

A Choice of Poets

Mystery Stories of the Nineteenth Century including The Signalman

Nineteenth Century Short Stories

Poetry of the First World War

Six Women Poets

Margaret Atwood
Cat's Eye
The Handmaid's Tale

Jane Austen
Emma
Mansfield Park
Persuasion
Pride and Prejudice
Sense and Sensibility

Alan Bennett
Talking Heads

William Blake
Songs of Innocence and of Experience

Charlotte Brontë
Jane Eyre
Villette

Emily Brontë
Wuthering Heights

Angela Carter
Nights at the Circus

Geoffrey Chaucer
The Franklin's Prologue and Tale
The Miller's Prologue and Tale
The Prologue to the Canterbury Tales
The Wife of Bath's Prologue and Tale

Samuel Coleridge
Selected Poems

Joseph Conrad
Heart of Darkness

Daniel Defoe
Moll Flanders

Charles Dickens
Bleak House
Great Expectations
Hard Times

Emily Dickinson
Selected Poems

John Donne
Selected Poems

Carol Ann Duffy
Selected Poems

George Eliot
Middlemarch
The Mill on the Floss

T.S. Eliot
Selected Poems
The Waste Land

F. Scott Fitzgerald
The Great Gatsby

E.M. Forster
A Passage to India

Brian Friel
Translations

Thomas Hardy
Jude the Obscure
The Mayor of Casterbridge
The Return of the Native
Selected Poems
Tess of the d'Urbervilles

Seamus Heaney
Selected Poems from 'Opened Ground'

Nathaniel Hawthorne
The Scarlet Letter

Homer
The Iliad
The Odyssey

Aldous Huxley
Brave New World

Kazuo Ishiguro
The Remains of the Day

Ben Jonson
The Alchemist

James Joyce
Dubliners

John Keats
Selected Poems

Christopher Marlowe
Doctor Faustus
Edward II

Arthur Miller
Death of a Salesman

John Milton
Paradise Lost Books I & II

Toni Morrison
Beloved

George Orwell
Nineteen Eighty-Four

Sylvia Plath
Selected Poems

Alexander Pope
Rape of the Lock & Selected Poems

William Shakespeare
Antony and Cleopatra
As You Like It
Hamlet
Henry IV Part I
King Lear
Macbeth
Measure for Measure
The Merchant of Venice
A Midsummer Night's Dream
Much Ado About Nothing
Othello
Richard II
Richard III
Romeo and Juliet
The Taming of the Shrew
The Tempest
Twelfth Night
The Winter's Tale

George Bernard Shaw
Saint Joan

Mary Shelley
Frankenstein

Jonathan Swift
Gulliver's Travels and A Modest Proposal

Alfred Tennyson
Selected Poems

Virgil
The Aeneid

Alice Walker
The Color Purple

Oscar Wilde
The Importance of Being Earnest

Tennessee Williams
A Streetcar Named Desire

Jeanette Winterson
Oranges Are Not the Only Fruit

John Webster
The Duchess of Malfi

Virginia Woolf
To the Lighthouse

W.B. Yeats
Selected Poems

Metaphysical Poets

THE ULTIMATE WEB SITE FOR THE ULTIMATE LITERATURE GUIDES

At York Notes we believe in helping you achieve exam success. Log on to **www.yorknotes.com** and see how we have made revision even easier, with over 300 titles available to download twenty-four hours a day. The downloads have lots of additional features such as pop-up boxes providing instant glossary definitions, user-friendly links to every part of the guide, and scanned illustrations offering visual appeal. All you need to do is log on to **www.yorknotes.com** and download the books you need to help you achieve exam success.

KEY FEATURES:

Details on how York Notes can help you

Menu Bar to help you find your way around the site

Details on how to download York Notes

Quick Search facility to help you find the titles you need

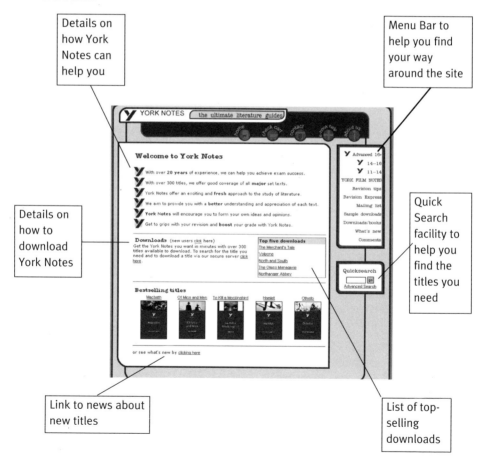

Link to news about new titles

List of top-selling downloads